Robert Boyte C. Howell

The early Baptists of Virginia

Robert Boyte C. Howell

The early Baptists of Virginia

ISBN/EAN: 9783743334588

Manufactured in Europe, USA, Canada, Australia, Japa

Cover: Foto ©ninafisch / pixelio.de

Manufactured and distributed by brebook publishing software
(www.brebook.com)

Robert Boyte C. Howell

The early Baptists of Virginia

THE

EARLY BAPTISTS OF VIRGINIA.

BY

ROBERT BOYLE C. HOWELL, D.D.,

Pastor of the Second Baptist Church, Richmond, Va.

Author of "TERMS OF COMMUNION," "THE DEACONSHIP," "THE WAY
OF SALVATION," "THE EVILS OF INFANT BAPTISM,"
"THE CROSS," "THE COVENANTS," &c.

———

PHILADELPHIA:

THE BIBLE AND PUBLICATION SOCIETY,

530 Arch Street.

Dedication.

—

To ARCHIBALD THOMAS, Esq.,

OF RICHMOND, VIRGINIA,

HIS EARLY, AND DURING FORTY YEARS, HIS UNWAVERING

AND DEARLY-LOVED FRIEND

AND BROTHER IN CHRIST,

THIS WORK IS RESPECTFULLY DEDICATED BY

THE AUTHOR.

RICHMOND, VIRGINIA,
June 10th, 1857.

PREFACE.

THE book which is here offered to the public is an enlargement of an Address delivered by Dr. Howell, in New York, in 1856, before the American Baptist Historical Society, and then published by the Society in pamphlet form. Soon after its publication, in 1857, he expanded it into a book, and a subsequent revision in 1864 gave it its present form. The interest which the original attempt to set forth the character and work of early Virginia Baptists excited, induces the hope that the present completer work may be received by Baptists everywhere as a valuable contribution to their history. It commends itself indeed to all students of history, and especially to the friends of religious liberty, as a careful delineation (drawn for the most part from original sources) of a part of one of the great movements of modern society.

1*

It is matter of regret that the learned and pious author is not permitted to witness the heightened interest which the Baptists of Virginia are showing in the great names and deeds of their past. No one would have felt deeper sympathy with, or taken more earnest part in, the memorial-movement than he, and none would have kept a praiseworthy denominational pride more free from narrow-minded or merely worldly sectarian feeling.

The book appears under the disadvantages of a posthumous work. If the author were living, he might choose to make additions or modifications; but his manuscript is printed as he left it, without alteration.

CONTENTS.

CHAPTER I.

CHAPTER IV.

BAPTIST PRINCIPLES IN VIRGINIA FIRST EMBODIED IN VISI-
BLE CHURCHES.

CHAPTER V.

PROGRESS OF BAPTIST PRINCIPLES IN VIRGINIA.

CHAPTER VI.

CAUSES OF BAPTIST SUCCESS IN VIRGINIA.

CHAPTER VII.

CONTROVERSIES OF THE EARLY BAPTISTS OF VIRGINIA.

CHAPTER VIII.

EPISCOPACY AMONG THE EARLY BAPTISTS OF VIRGINIA.

CHAPTER IX.

CHAPTER X.

CHAPTER XI.

CHAPTER XII.

CHAPTER XIII.

EARLY BAPTISTS OF VIRGINIA.

CHAPTER I.

INTRODUCTORY.

Virginia Baptist history unwritten. Injustice to the memory of the Early Baptists, by both friends and enemies. Sources of information regarding them. A sketch of their principles. Influence of these principles upon other denominations. Present condition of Baptists in Virginia. Design of the present work.

THE pride of ancestry is a natural and commendable passion. It is cherished with enthusiasm by both families and nations. Nor is it surprising that into this spirit churches also warmly enter. He must be strangely constituted who feels no interest in the character of his progenitors. In their honor, every man must be conscious that he is a partaker. From their shame, who does not involuntarily shrink? To this general principle, in its application to churches, the Baptists of Virginia seem to have formed a marked exception. Never has a class of men existed who were more devoted, laborious, self-sacrificing, disinterested, and successful than were the fathers of this State. Not one century, however, has passed away, and already they are nearly forgotten, even by their own ecclesiastical children! This injustice to a large

11

and influential class of her people is not characteristic of Virginia as a State. "To make familiar to the popular mind whatever concerns her greatness and honor, every form of intellectual communication has been exhausted. Song and oration, history and novel, have been full of her glory. Her chivalry and her statesmanship, her arts and her letters, her power and her resources, have brought into requisition the talents and scholarship of her most illustrious sons. Volume after volume has been laid upon her literary altars, evincing the warmest devotion to the interests of her people, to her honor as a State, and demonstrating her distinguished position in the great American Confederacy." Nor have any of the other leading denominations been wanting in able, learned, and enthusiastic historians. The History of the Baptists of Virginia remains unwritten! Poetry has not enshrined their exalted deeds. Literature has raised no worthy monument to commemorate their name and virtues.

It is true that Ashland and Leland, Edwards and Gano, Burkitt and Read, Backus and Benedict, Semple and Taylor, have written Chronicles of the Early Baptists of Virginia, but they are exceedingly brief, fragmentary, and imperfect, and some of them have not even been published. Separately they are of little value, and collectively they embody only a few of those facts which they found floating upon the surface of public knowledge, and even these they have thrown together with little arrangement or discrimination. The injury done to their fame by this carelessness of their friends, has been greatly aggravated by the misrepre-

sentations of their ecclesiastical opponents. Jarrett
and Burke, White and Hawks, Foote and Meade, and
a few others, have published Annals, more or less full
and pretentious, of their several denominations. It is
impossible, however, to read these works without feeling deep regret that the prejudices and aversion of
these writers were permitted so fully to control all their
statements regarding Baptist people, and Baptist principles. Their strange distortions of the facts in history
are, it is believed, to be attributed rather to their ignorance of the subject upon which it was their business to treat, than to any deliberate purpose to mislead
the public mind. However this may be, these several
works, so far as they refer to the Baptists, are wholly
unworthy of their distinguished authors.

Ample materials for a full and faithful history of
the Baptists of Virginia are accessible. They can be
obtained, however, only by laborious, persevering, and
well directed investigations. To some of them reference has already been made, in the several books indicated. Others will be collected in the form of pamphlets; and the correspondence of the first churches,
and especially those south of James River, with
churches and brethren in the city of London; and the
records of various denominational proceedings, in Europe and America. But the richest repositories, and
those which still remain almost wholly unexplored,
are the records of the Courts in the several counties,
before which at various times they were arraigned on
account of their religion, and by the orders of which
they were fined, imprisoned, and otherwise severely

2

punished; their memorials and other communications, addressed to the State Convention, and subsequently to the General Assembly; the "Complimentary Answers," and other records, found in the Journals of these bodies; the laws of the Colony and the State, as embodied in "The Revised Laws of Virginia;" "Hening's Statutes at Large," "The Code of Virginia," and other books of like character; "The Works of Thomas Jefferson," the papers of James Madison, many of which are published in "The Federalist;" their several memorials to Congress, and its proceedings regarding them; and their correspondence, official and unofficial, with Washington and Jefferson, during the period in which these gentlemen occupied the chair of President of the United States. The proper exploration of these sources of knowledge will open to the industrious investigator numerous others. With such materials, why may not some Baptist Irving, Prescott, or Bancroft soon produce a history worthy of the exalted character, and distinguished labors and successes, of the Baptists of Virginia? To write such a work is no part of my present purpose. Imperative professional duties, which cannot be intermitted, leave me, even if I possessed the necessary genius and skill, no time for such an employment. All that I shall attempt will be to ascertain to what extent the Baptist element existed among the early colonists in Virginia; the time and circumstances, under which Baptist principles were embodied among them in visible churches; the subsequent extraordinary progress of these principles among the people; the principal causes that facilitated their advancement; the controversies that prevailed among the Baptists, and their harmonious adjustment; the political doctrines which they maintained; the influence they exercised in the formation of the government of the State, and of the United States; and the position, social, intellectual, and moral, of their ministers and people in the Commonwealth. The period within which I shall confine myself, is that which commences with the settlement of the English Colony at Jamestown, and closes with the termination of the eighteenth century.

One very important advantage contemplated in the execution of this purpose is the presentation of a sketch at least, and in a form indisputably authentic, of those peculiar principles by which in all ages and countries Baptists have been invariably distinguished. In our day, and in this country, so many of these great principles have been adopted by other denominations, that the masses have ceased to remember that they ever were peculiarly Baptist, and are accustomed publicly to proclaim, that Baptists differ from others mainly, if not exclusively, as to "the mode, and subjects of baptism; and perhaps in some unimportant matters relating to church organization and polity!" Nor have Baptists themselves cared to correct this injurious mistake! On the topics indicated, they do indeed stand alone; but these form, in reality, a very small, and by no means the most important, part of their peculiarities. These doctrines may, it is believed, be summarily set forth thus:

The Bible is the only rule of faith and obedience;

regeneration and sanctification are the work of the Holy Spirit, in the heart of the believer; justification is exclusively by the grace of God, through faith in our Lord Jesus Christ; holy living is the only conclusive proof of real discipleship to Christ; membership in the churches is confined strictly to the professedly regenerate; all ministers are, as to office, the equals of each other; a church is a single congregation of believers, meeting in one place, maintaining uncorrupted the doctrines and ordinances of the gospel; each individual church is free, no power, ecclesiastical or civil, outside of itself, having over it any authority or rule whatever: baptism and the Lord's Supper are always declaratory of the previous faith of the recipient; the churches and the State are, as such, entirely separate, and neither can legislate for the other; every man has an inalienable right to perfect freedom of conscience and worship; and all are entitled to the full and equal protection of the government under which they live, in the exercise of all their rights, political, social, and religious. These, it is believed, embrace the outlines of the Baptist faith peculiarly. As a whole and in its several parts, it clearly bears the stamp and seal of Almighty God. He who embraces these views is, in principle, necessarily a Baptist. No church that departs from them can long remain evangelical. No State that fails in its civil government to concede and act upon them, ever can be free.

From the time of the subversion of the churches under the iron rule of Constantine the Great, to the period of the American revolution, all these principles were, with some slight modifications, repudiated and denounced by every prevalent class of Christians; and the few who attempted to maintain them publicly did so at the risk of their reputation, their fortune, and their life. Many a martyr has expired on the gibbet and in the flames, whose only crime was the love and support of these great and fundamental principles! The modifications alluded to had reference to the leaders in the Reformation of the sixteenth century. The Lutheran, the Calvinist, and the English Churches, and, through their overshadowing influence, some of the minor sects, nominally embraced some few of these tenets. They admitted in theory, but ignored in practice, the sufficiency of the word of God, as the only rule of faith and obedience; they attributed the work of regeneration to the Holy Ghost, but maintained that he accomplished it only through the ordinance of baptism; and they taught justification by faith alone; but the remainder they repudiated and opposed. Especially did they denounce all those which guard the purity of the churches, and their Scriptural polity; their separation from the civil government; the freedom of conscience and worship; and the right of every citizen, whatever his religion, to the full and equal protection of the government, in his person, property, and political immunities. These and such like doctrines were no less offensive to the Reformers, than they were to the Roman Catholics. The natural results have been, that all these churches have gradually fallen back into nearly all the corruptions from which for a season they had escaped. The Presbyterian and Congregational Churches, bodies which sprang out of the German Reformation; some classes of Episcopalians; and the Methodist Church—an offshoot of English Episcopacy, have, in a great measure, been saved from a like deterioration only by their contact with the Baptist churches and people, and their practical adoption of so many of the principles by which they have ever been distinguished. Their practice approximates them to Baptists, and counteracts to a gratifying extent the evils inherent in their doctrinal principles.

Every good man must rejoice that now at length the Virginia Baptist Fathers are beginning to attract, to a much greater extent than heretofore, the attention of the Christian world. Not much longer, it is hoped, will they remain without a memorial worthy of their exalted character. When such a memorial is written it will afford another eminent illustration of the power of simple gospel truth over the hearts of men; its sufficiency to sweep away error, no matter how inveterate and venerable; and of the facility, when left to its own influence, with which it moulds governments, ecclesiastical and civil, to the principles of freedom and justice. If in these pages I shall be able to contribute somewhat to such a work, my design will have been fully accomplished.

CHAPTER II.

BAPTIST ELEMENT AMONG THE EARLY COLONISTS OF VIRGINIA.

Intolerance in the Old World towards Baptist principles. Increasing number of Baptists. The violence of their persecution. The New World an asylum. The presence of Baptists in the other colonies. The number and condition of Baptist Churches in London, and its neighborhood. The soldiers of Cromwell's Army who escaped to Virginia. Virginia a place of concealment for the persecuted. The emigration of Baptists from Virginia to North Carolina.

THE early colonists in Virginia were gathered from all classes of the people of England. That there were Baptists among them we have no direct official testimony, but the circumstantial proofs of their presence are full and conclusive. To evince the correctness of this statement, we will in the first place sketch the condition of religious society in the Old World, and especially with reference to Baptists and Baptist principles, for some time previous to the settlement of the Colony at Jamestown, and during the remainder or the seventeenth century.

The prevalence of Baptists in most of the nations of Europe, and especially in Britain, from the earliest times and in no very small numbers, will be questioned by no one who is at all familiar with the religious history of the land of our forefathers. The doctrines which they invariably held were equally well known. To the despots of the world, religious and political, they have ever been, and continue to be, unmeasurably

offensive. Hence, in Europe, Baptists have been denounced by all churches, Catholic and Protestant, and
by all civil governments. By all, their doctrines have
been authoritatively declared to be "blasphemy against
God, and treason against the State." All, therefore,
who dared to profess and practice them, were at once
declared infamous, and placed without the protection
of the laws, and with fire and sword hunted from the
world. These facts are all fully attested by historians
of every class, and no less clearly by their enemies,
such as Fuller and Mosheim and Milner and Nean-
der, than by their friends, Jones and Irving, Choules,
Neal, Anderson, Orchard, and Underhill.* The
movements of the Baptists were traceable everywhere
by the blood and gibbets and fires with which their
persecutors pursued them.

The civil commotions of England which immediately
preceded the planting of the Virginia colony gave
some respite to the Baptists ; their numbers, therefore,
multiplied ; and ever and anon churches sprang up,
both in the capital and throughout the country. Of
their character and numbers, and the spirit with
which they bore their persecutions, the distinguished
President of the Council of Trent bears unwonted testimony. He says, "If you behold their cheerfulness
in suffering persecution, the Anabaptists run before all
others. If you have regard to their number, it is like

---

* Had the author been writing at the present day he would not
have failed to insert the name of Dr. J. M. Cramp, whose "Baptist
History" was issued by the American Baptist Publication Society
after the preparation of the present work.—EDITOR.

that in multitude they would swarm above all others, if they were not grievously plagued and cut off with the knife of persecution. If you have an eye to the outward appearance of godliness, both the Lutherans and Zwinglians must needs grant that they far pass them." *   " The Roman Catholics," says Underhill, † "abhorred the Baptists, for if this heresy prevailed, a church hoary with age, laden with the spoils of many lands, and rich in the merchandise of souls, must be broken down and destroyed. The Protestants hated them, for if they triumphed, then their cherished headship, their worldly alliances, the pomps and circumstances of their state religion, must be debased before the kingly crown of Jesus. The Puritans loathed them, for Baptist sentiments are too liberal for those who seek a papal authority over conscience, and the sword of the temporal power to enforce their ' Holy Discipline.' " They have all sought the destruction of the Baptists, "because from the beginning they have," as the great Locke justly affirms, " been the advocates and friends of absolute liberty ; just and true liberty ; equal and impartial liberty."

In that age Papists and Protestants, who between them ruled the nations of Europe, furiously and by every possible means destroyed each other. Than these, never were enemies more bitter or relentless. In one thing however, and one only, they were agreed: they zealously united all their powers for

* Religious Liberty, its Struggles and Triumphs.—Underhill, pp. 88, 89.

† Ibid. 201. (In substance.)

the extermination of the Baptists. Not one of them which either party could reach ever escaped. In several of the treaties between the Catholic and Protestant States, special articles were inserted, as will be seen by examining their National Records, binding both parties to destroy, as far as possible, this hated class of men. Of the manner in which these engagements were fulfilled by the Protestants, D'Aubigne, the distinguished Historian of the Reformation, may be consulted. He says:—"Accordingly Luther, on his return from Wittenberg, extinguished in Germany the fanaticism of the Anabaptists." * The miseries, murders, and desolations, which accompanied this *extinguishment*, are detailed in the Dutch and other Martyrologies recently published in England by the Hansard Knollys Society. The Auto da Fes of the Catholics, in which so many Baptists perished, were perhaps not exceeded in atrocity by the fiendish butcheries which they suffered throughout Germany, at the hands of Luther and his disciples.

Nor were the Protestants content when they had "extinguished in *Germany* the fanaticism of the Anabaptists." They pursued them with cruel malignity into other countries. "The princes of Germany," says Dr. Cox,† "having discovered by means of intercepted letters, a secret correspondence between the German and English Anabaptists, wrote an epistle to Henry VIII., containing a statement of their pernicious doctrines, and warning him of danger likely to

---

* Hist. Ref. Vol. 3, p. 305.
† Life of Melancthon, p. 218.

result from their fanatical proceedings, unless prevented by a bold and timely interference." This "epistle of the princes," was, as we are specifically informed, advised by Luther, and written at their request by Melancthon. It was the united work of the leading German Protestants. Its effect upon Henry is indicated by the proceedings of an Ecclesiastical Convention, assembled in compliance with the king's order, in 1530, by Warham, Archbishop of Canterbury, in which many of the peculiar doctrines of the Baptists were formally condemned, and all of them pronounced by authority, "damnable heresies." Two proclamations immediately followed, directing the apprehension of all persons accused of being Baptists, and ordering the severest punishment to be inflicted upon all who should be convicted of that horrible crime. These processes were directed "against the malicious sects of heretics who, by perversion of Holy Scripture, do induce erroneous opinions, sow dissensions among Christian people, and finally disturb the peace and tranquility of Christian realms, as lately happened in some parts of Germany." * To what extent Henry and his successors on the British throne carried these persecutions, the prisons of the United Kingdom and the fires of Smithfield bear the amplest testimony.

The sentiments and practice of Calvin and his disciples regarding the Baptists are well known to have been in perfect consonance with those of the German and English princes and divines. This is sufficiently evinced by the martyrdoms which by his concurrence

* Struggles and Triumphs, &c., p. 92.

were inflicted even in Geneva itself. The learned
Boyle has justly said, "Not a Reformer of any emi-
nence can be named who did not take part in this
crusade [against the Baptists.] Luther, Melancthon,
Zwingle, Bucer, Bullinger, Calvin, and others abroad ;
at home, Cranmer, Latimer, Ridley, Philpot, Becon,
Turner, and many others." *

During the reign of Elizabeth, the Baptists in
England, to defend themselves against the defamation
of their enemies, ventured to publish an unpretending
treatise, in which they summoned boldness to protest
against "Persecutions for conscience' sake." In that
work they maintained the following great principles:—
"According to the word of God, Christ is the Supreme
Head of his church; the Queen has no right to frame
ecclesiastical laws, nor to appoint ministers of religion;
the Church ought to be composed of believers only ;
the baptism of infants is unlawful." These annun-
ciations shocked insufferably all parties. John Knox
himself, the father of Scotch and British Presbyterians, responded in a work entitled, "An answer to a
great number of cavillations, written by an Anabap-
tist Adversary." It must ever be regretted that a
man, so excellent in many respects as was Knox, permitted himself in this volume to apply the bitterest
epithets to those whom he chooses to regard as his
adversaries, and to denounce them in the most unmea-
sured terms. He closes his book in the following language, addressed to the writer of the treatises referred
to:—"It is my full purpose to lay the same to thy

* Dictionary, Art. Anabap. note B.

charge, if I shall apprehend thee in any commonwealth where justice against blasphemers may be
ministered according to God's word."

As on the continent of Europe Catholics and Protestants were agreed in persecuting the Baptists, so in
Britain Episcopalians and Presbyterians, in all else
irreconcilable enemies, concurred and co-operated in
every possible measure for their extermination. Scotch
Presbyters and English Bishops suffered at the hands of
each other every possible injury which one could inflict
upon the other. Many a time in our early years have
we been moved to tears by the recital, in books skil-
fully prepared for children, of the sufferings of Covenanters, but no allusions were made to the miseries
these very Covenanters inflicted upon the Baptists of
their day. We have wept in our youth over the hard
fate of Cranmer and Ridley and Rogers and others,
who under the reign of bloody Mary fell martyrs by
the hands of the Papists. Who that does not know the
facts would suspect that these were the very men who
under the preceding reign were the most zealous and
active in arresting Baptists and sending them to be
burned at the stake. Neal's History of the Puritans *
discloses many melancholy transactions, evincing their
deep guilt as persecutors, and showing that the
sufferings which at last overtook them bore many of
the features of a just and righteous retribution. The
formidable multiplication of Baptists about this period,
to which we have before referred, and the rapidly
growing popularity of their peculiar doctrines with

* Choules' edit. N. Y. Vol. 2, pp. 352—380.

3

the masses of the people, greatly irritated the English government. Laws were therefore enacted, " Commanding the most rigid search for them throughout the kingdom, with a view to the utter extermination of this hated sect." A " Commission " for the purpose was appointed, at the head of which stood the great names of Cranmer and Ridley, both of whom executed their bloody office, not only without relentings, but with singular ferocity. For proof and illustration of these facts, a single example shall suffice. Joan of Kent, a distinguished and noble lady, was the first Baptist arrested under this new authority. With very little ceremony or delay, she was convicted as a heretic, and sentenced to be burned alive at the stake. To consummate this horrible judicial murder, it was necessary, in compliance with the law, that the sentence of the court should be approved by the king. The amiable and youthful Edward was now upon the throne. The victim of these cruel prelates was well known to him as one among the best and most estimable of women. He therefore refused his assent. He would not sign her death warrant. Cranmer was deputed by his associates to go to the young king, and to persuade him to comply with their decision. His arguments are recorded by the historian. Two of them may be mentioned. He assumed that Joan was a blasphemer, and maintained the justice of the sentence against her from the law of Moses, according to which all blasphemers were commanded to be stoned; and he enforced the obligation of Edward to approve their sentence, ordering her to the stake, by the con-

sideration, that there are impieties against God which
princes as his deputies are obliged to punish, among
which blasphemy holds the highest place, just as the
king's deputies are obliged to punish offences against
the king's person. The young monarch, says Bur-
net,* heard him long and patiently, and, "rather
silenced than convinced" by his argument, "he set his
hand to the warrant with tears in his eyes, telling
Cranmer, that if he did wrong, as he signed it only in
submission to his authority, he (Cranmer) should answer for it to God." And indeed, soon and sternly
did he answer for it to God.

John Rogers, too, and in this very case, was not less
criminally implicated than Archbishop Cranmer. A
distinguished gentleman, whose name is not mentioned
by the annalists, shocked by the cruelty about to be
inflicted upon a lady, illustrious in both birth and
character, and well knowing the influence of Rogers
with the governing powers, sought an interview with
him, and earnestly entreated him to do what he could
to save her life, or at least to procure for her a less
dreadful death than burning at the stake. This proud
priest evinced on the whole subject the coldest indifference, and in answer simply remarked, "The woman
ought to be put to death;" and "Burning alive is not
a cruel death, but easy enough!" Astonished at this
answer, which showed so little regard for the sufferings
of others, the gentleman striking the hand of Rogers,
which up to that time he had held firmly grasped in
his own, replied with great vehemence, "Well, proba-

* History of the Reformation, vol. 2, p. 110.

bly it may so happen that you yourself will one day have your hands full of this mild burning." And so indeed, in the providence of God, it did happen. These men died, but not one of them more unjustly nor more cruelly than did the multitudes of Baptist victims they had themselves so relentlessly destroyed.

In the facts now submitted, we have a rapid sketch of the religious condition of the Old World, with reference to Baptist principles, for some time before and during the period of the planting of the Virginia Colony. Finding no place in Europe where they could be secure from the hand of violence; groaning under oppressions of every kind; hunted perpetually by the most malignant persecutors; and a broad land in the New World open before them, having the aspect of an asylum, and inviting their residence,—is it reasonable to conclude that there were no Baptists among the thousands of colonists who so eagerly flocked to Jamestown?

The other American colonies, I observe in the second place, were well known to have contained Baptists, and in no very inconsiderable numbers, especially Massachusetts, Rhode Island, and Pennsylvania. Speaking of the German Baptists, from whom their British brethren did not differ in sentiment, and erroneously imagining that they all sprang up with the great Christian leaders of the Reformation, Bancroft, who cherishes no sympathy with the Baptists' religious system, aside from its political aspects, in his History of the United States,* eloquently says: — "With

* Vol. 2, p. 457.

greater consistency than Luther, they applied the doctrines of the Reformation to the social positions of life, and threatened an end to priestcraft and kingcraft, spiritual dominations, tythes, and vassalage. The party (English Baptists) was trodden under foot with foul reproaches, most arrogant scorn; and its history is written in the blood of myriads of the German (and English) peasantry; but its principles secure in their immortality, escaped with Roger Williams and his colony to Rhode Island, to witness that naturally the paths of the Baptists are paths of freedom, of pleasantness, and peace." In Massachusetts, where "*the Lords Brethren*" of the Congregationalists, copied so closely the spirit and conduct of "*the Lords Bishops*" *of the English Episcopalians*, the presence of the Baptists is testified by the persecuting edicts fulminated against them by the government, and the records of courts which dragged them to prison, harassed them with fines, and in the public places scourged them with stripes. Thence they fled to Rhode Island, to Pennsylvania, and to both the Carolinas. Did none of them find their way to the secluded glens and sunny valleys of Virginia, the oldest, if not the best, of all the American colonies? If not, how can we account for a fact so extraordinary?

The colony at Jamestown, it must be noticed in the third place, was mostly settled by immigrants from London and its neighborhood under the proprietorship and superintendence of "The London Company." The nobility and gentry, who formed a portion of their number so inconveniently large as to elicit on several

occasions the complaints of the Colonial Governors,
were ambitious especially to acquire for themselves
large bodies of land in Virginia, such as those possessed by the princes, dukes, and other aristocratic
houses of "The Mother State." Nor did they entirely fail of their purpose. Fairfax, Byrd, Spotts-
wood, and many others, rejoiced in domains not inferior
in extent to some of the German Principalities, and to
several of the subsequent States, such as Rhode Island,
Delaware, or New Jersey. These proprietors were
anxious to settle their " Plantations" with a virtuous
and industrious peasantry, into the religious opinions
of whom, other things being satisfactory, they are not
likely to inquire very closely. Private adventurers
also and small capitalists came in large numbers, who
sought a livelihood by other means than vassalage to
the great. Through various authorities, such as Irving, Underhill, and the Preface to the Philadelphia
Confession of Faith, we ascertain that at the period of
which we now write, there were certainly in the very
places from which these immigrants came—London
and its neighborhood—more than a hundred Baptist
churches. Did the tide flowing to the west with so
much power carry none of them to Virginia? Such a
conclusion is necessarily wholly incredible.

On the restoration to the throne of England, we
observe in the fourth place, of the second Charles,
great numbers, as is well known, of Cromwell's vete-
ran soldiers escaped to Virginia. Of these soldiers
Dr. Williams says:*—" The period of the Common-

* Life and Times of Baxter—in The Christian Review.

wealth and the Protectorate was the season in which our distinguishing sentiments, hitherto the hidden treasure of a few solitary confessors, became the property of the people. Through weary years they had been held by a few, in deep retirement, and at the peril of their lives. Now they began rapidly working their way, and openly into the masses of society. The army which won for Cromwell his 'crowning mercies,' as he called those splendid victories which secured the power of the Parliament, became deeply tinged with our views of faith and order. They were not, as military bodies have so often been, a band of mercenary hirelings—the sweepings of society, gleaned from the alehouse and the kennel, or snatched from the jail, and due to the gallows—but they were composed chiefly of substantial yeomanry, men who entered the ranks for principle rather than for gain, and whose chief motive for enlistment was that they believed the impending contest to be one for religious truth and for the national liberties; a war in the strictest sense *pro aris et focis.* Clarendon himself allows their superiority in morals and character to the royalist forces. In this army the officers were many of them accustomed to preach; and both commanders and privates were continually busied in searching the Scriptures, in prayer, and in Christian conference. The result of the Biblical studies and free communings of these intrepid, high-principled men, was that they became, a large portion of them, Baptists. As to their character, the splendid eulogy they won from Milton may counterbalance the coarse caricatures of poets and novelists, who saw them less closely, and disliked their piety too strongly, to judge dispassionately of their merits."

These were the men so many of whom were Baptists, and who in numbers so large found a refuge from the malignity of kings and bishops in the Virginia colony. And in his History of the Protestant Episcopal Church in Virginia,* has not Dr. Hawks his eye upon these very men when he says:—"The assemblages, (in Virginia about this time—1680), there is reason to believe, were perverted from religious to treasonable purposes;" that in these professedly religious meetings "they concocted among the sectaries of their creeds the subversion of the government;" and that four men of their number "were vilely hung as a warning to the remainder!" These charges and proceedings are strongly suggestive. They resemble, to a painful extent, those had against Baptists in England, who, because they dared to express their own religious opinions, were denounced as rebels, condemned as felons, and executed as traitors to their country.

It is proper, in the fifth place, to state, which we do upon the authority of Graham, in his "History of the United States," † that there were, at a very early period, "Puritans" in the colony of Virginia; and that there were Quakers there also, is shown by the law of "The Grand Assembly" adopted at its session of 1661, for the suppression in the colony of that eccentric sect.‡ Also that "Non-conformists" were

---

* Pp. 71, 72.   † Vol. I. p. 219.
‡ Hening's Statutes at Large, vol. I. Journals of the Legislature of 1661.

present is evinced by similar laws in regard to them. And were there no Baptists there?

From Morgan Edwards and others, it may in the last place be stated, we learn some facts of unquestionable truth, entirely to our purpose. It is of record, that as early as 1695, numerous Baptists were found residing in the lower and northern parts of North Carolina. Most of these, we are told, had gone over to that colony from contiguous portions of Virginia, to escape the intolerance of her ecclesiastical laws.*

Let all the facts now submitted be weighed attentively; the intolerance exercised towards their religion in the Old World; their gradually augmenting numbers; the violence of the persecutions constantly waged against them in England; their presence in the other American colonies; the number and condition of Baptist churches in London and its neighborhood, which supplied most of the colonists for Jamestown; the large number of Cromwell's soldiers, so many of whom were Baptists, who on the restoration of Charles the Second escaped to this colony; the asylum which Virginia might be presumed to afford to the persecuted; and the emigration of the Baptists from this colony to North Carolina, and the conclusion to my mind is irresistible, that from its very beginning the Baptist element prevailed to no small extent among the colonists of Virginia.

* Sketches of Virginia and North Carolina. Comer's Journal. Benedict, vol. 2, p. 97.

CHAPTER III.

CAUSES WHICH DELAYED THE ORGANIZATION OF BAPTIST CHURCHES IN VIRGINIA.

The government of the Virginia Colony. Rule of the London Company. The Episcopal Church established in the colony. Laws enforcing religious conformity. Instances of persecution. Intimidation of the people.

A FULL century had passed away, from the time of the settlement at Jamestown, and Baptist principles still remained in Virginia, unembodied in any visible churches. Professors of that faith were unquestionably in the colony during all this period. They were not careless in their morals, nor forgetful of the value of their cherished doctrines. We have seen that essays had been made to hold religious assemblies, and that these assemblies had been charged with plotting treason against the government under the pretence of religion, had been violently dispersed, and their leaders hung as a warning to their associates. We have also seen that these people were probably Baptists, since the offences charged against them were the same alleged against Baptists in Europe, and for which they had there uniformly similarly been punished; that with such warnings and the laws enacted to repress all religious sentiments not in concord with the Church of England, some of which we shall presently consider, it is not surprising that they were so long deterred from attempting any open religious organizations.

The colonists of Jamestown were of a character altogether different from those of Plymouth. They were, indeed, although from the same parent country, essentially, two races of men. The people of the north—at first known as Northern Virginia, but afterwards as Massachusetts—were Puritans of the Cromwellian school, and inveterate Congregationalists. Some of them, before they crossed the Atlantic, had fled from England, and had for years resided in Holland. They were rough, determined, intrepid, and their religion partook largely of the elements of pride and fanaticism. The people of the South were Cavaliers, soft, polished, courtly, proud in their manner; loyal in the highest degree to the English government; not austere; nor scrupulous in their personal religion; but more intolerant of any departures from its external forms than were their Puritan neighbors. The men of the North abjured the Church of England, from whose power and tyranny they had with difficulty escaped. The men of the South profoundly venerated the Church of England, brought it with them to their western home, and cherished and guarded it with sleepless vigilance. In the South and in the North the people were equally solicitous as to the means of education. Next to their churches their schools shared most largely in their attentions. The first school of any pretensions which originated in Virginia—and this was amply endowed with immense bodies of valuable land—was "The University of Henrico," which was located near the site now occupied by the city of Richmond. The next was "The Free Academy," which had its locality in Charles-city County. Both these schools were subsequently merged in "The College of William and Mary," at Williamsburg, the capital of the colony. From that time forward, and up to a very recent period, that College was the pride and honor of Virginia. It bears to-day, upon the catalogue of its graduates, a larger number of names distinguished in the various walks of life, than perhaps any other similar institution in America. Such were the people of the colony of Virginia.

The first charter of the colony was granted by James the First, and was dated April 10th, 1606. It was, for the time being, the organic law. That part of the law which refers to religion is as follows :

"We do specially ordain, charge, and require the said Presidents, and Councils, and the Ministers of the said several colonies respectively, within their limits and precincts, that they with all diligence, care, and respect do provide that the true word and service of God, and Christian faith, be preached, planted, and used, not only within every of the said several colonies and plantations, but also as much as they may among the savage people which do or shall adjoin unto them, according to the doctrine, rites, and religion now professed, and established within our realm of England ; and that they shall not suffer any person or persons, to withdraw any of the subjects or people inhabiting or who shall inhabit within any of the said several colonies and plantations from the same, or from their due allegiance to us and our heirs and successors, as their immediate sovereign under God; and if they shall find within the said colonies and plantations any person or persons so seeking to withdraw any of the subjects of us, our heirs, or successors, or any of the people of these lands or territories within the precincts aforesaid, they shall with all diligence, him or them so offending cause to be apprehended, arrested, and imprisoned, until he shall fully and throughly reform himself; or otherwise, when the cause so requireth, that he shall with all convenient speed, be sent into our realm of England, here to receive condign punishment for his or their said offence or offences."*

By this charter, it will be seen that the Episcopal Church was established as the religion of the colony; that every subject or person was as much bound in allegiance to the Episcopal Church, as he was to the government of the king; that a withdrawal from the Episcopal Church and a revolt against the government are offences equally criminal; that all who should be found seeking to withdraw persons from the doctrine, rites, and religion of the Episcopal Church should be apprehended, arrested, and imprisoned; that the only condition of their release, should be their full and thorough reform; that in case they could not establish satisfactorily their full and thorough reformation, they should be sent prisoners to England, there to receive condign punishment; and that all Presidents, Councils, and Ministers were required with all diligence and

---

* Hening's Statutes at Large, vol. 1, pp. 68, 69.

4

care to execute this law, in its full extent and meaning.
With such a platform upon which to proceed in their
legislation, it may readily be imagined that the details
of Ecclesiastical law would be stringent to the last
degree. This conclusion with respect to the charter
is sustained by reference to "The Code of Sir Thomas
Dale," designed to direct in the details of its administration, the first published for the government of the
colony, and which bears date 1611. In regard to religion, this Code provides as follows:

"There is not one man nor woman in this colony,
now present nor hereafter to arrive, but shall give up
an account of his or their faith and religion, and repair
unto the minister, that by his conference with them,
he may understand and gather whether they have
been sufficiently instructed and catechised in the
principles and grounds of religion; whose weakness
and ignorance, the minister finding, and advising them
in love and charity to repair often unto him, to receive therein a greater measure of knowledge, if they
shall refuse to repair unto him, and he, the minister,
give notice thereof to the governor, or the chief officers
of that town or fort, wherein he or she, the parties so
offending shall remain, the governor shall cause the
offender for the first time of refusal, to be whipped;
for the second time, to be whipped twice, and to acknowledge his fault upon the Sabbath-day in the congregation; and for the third time, to be whipped every
day, until he hath made the same acknowledgment,
and asked forgiveness for the same, and shall repair
unto the minister to be further instructed as aforesaid;

and upon the Sabbath when the minister shall catechise, and demand any question concerning his faith
and knowledge, he shall not refuse to make answer,
upon the same peril."*

The very severity of these, and similar laws which
continued to be enacted during the administration of
the government of the colony by "The London Company," was perhaps their best antidote. They were indeed promulgated and constantly reiterated in the hear-
ing of the people in the "towns and forts," but in their
extreme features they were seldom executed. The in-
tentions of their rulers were, no doubt, sufficiently earnest, but they were, to a great extent, frustrated by the
circumstances of society and the temper of the people.

These laws of the Protestant colony of Virginia
contrast strangely, in some respects, with the laws of
the Roman Catholic colony of Maryland on the same
subject. By a law of the Maryland Colony of 1649,
it was provided :

"That no persons professing to believe in Jesus
Christ, should be molested in their religion, or in the
free exercise thereof, or be compelled to the exercise of
any other religion against their consent, so that they
be not unfaithful to the Proprietary, or conspire
against the civil Government; that any person molest-
ing another in respect of his religious tenets should pay
triple damages to the party aggrieved, and twenty
shillings to the Proprietary; that those reproaching
any with opprobrious names of religious distinction,
should forfeit ten shillings to the person injured."

* Laws, &c., Strachey, London, 1612.

Had this law terminated here, it would have been admirable indeed ; but unhappily it did not. It goes on to enact,—

"That any one speaking reproachfully against the Blessed Virgin, should forfeit ten pounds ; but that blasphemy against God should be punished with death."*

In Virginia, no religious offence, as such, was punished with death, but religious departure from the Church was treason against the State, and that was punished with, and non-conformity was visited by, a penalty little less severe, indefinite imprisonment, or banishment from the country, or transportation to England to receive "condign punishment." As to liberty of conscience and freedom of worship, Catholic Maryland was much more liberal than Protestant Virginia.

Fortunately for the Virginia colony, the Code of a Governor did not govern his successor, and Governor Dale was succeeded by men who regarded corporal punishment in another light, and were not so ready to resort to the lash on every occasion. As in the government of England for many centuries, the laws of a king died with him, and were not in force unless re-enacted by his successor, so with the Governor of Virginia. Every new Governor invariably brought with him his own "Code," which wholly superseded that of his predecessor. This continued to be the rule even after the organization of "The Grand Assembly." "It was a mode of legislation, "says Hen-

* Benedict's Hist. Bapt. Edit. 1813, vol. 2, p. 22.

ing, speaking of that body * peculiar to those times, to repeal all former laws, and re-enact them in the very words in which they were originally passed." The attention given to ecclesiastical affairs by the governors we have already seen. "The Grand Assembly was even more prolific than they were, of laws on the same subject. On this topic the learned jurist just named remarks: "If we may judge by the subject matter of such Acts as have been preserved, the legislature was exclusively occupied in promoting a uniformity to the doctrines and discipline of the Church of England, and in enforcing attendance at church, and other religious exercises."† We may here glance rapidly at some of these proceedings. ‡

By the Act of 1623, it was provided, that "In every plantation or settlement, there shall be a house or room, set apart for the worship of God," which worship was commanded and required to be "strictly in accordance with the constitution and canons of the Church of England." To administer in these several places, clergymen were employed by the government of the colony, and their salaries paid by a tax upon the people, levied and collected, as were the taxes for other colonial purposes. By the Act of 1643, entitled "An Act to preserve the purity of doctrine and unity of the Church," it was required, that "All ministers shall be conformable to the Orders and Constitution of the Church of England; that no others shall be permitted to teach or preach, publicly or privately," and

---

* Statutes at Large, vol. 1, p. 120.   † Statutes as above.
‡ Vide Statutes, &c., vol. 1, throughout.

that "the Governor and Council shall take care that all non-conformists depart the colony with all conveniency." The Legislature during the same session, adopted the "Statute of England" of 3d James I, "Concerning Popish Recusants," and put it into full and vigorous force in Virginia. During the session of 1657, laws of the severest character were enacted for the suppression of the Quakers in the colony. In the legislative attention of the session of 1661, "The Church" shared very largely. The first nine of its Acts had exclusive regard to ecclesiastical interests. It was provided in these laws that a church should be built and a vestry appointed in each parish in the colony; that "a Glebe with convenient houses built thereon" should be purchased by the colony for the minister of each parish; that ministers should receive for their salaries each, beside the glebe and its products, eighty pounds sterling—about four hundred dollars annually, which salary was by subsequent enactments changed to sixteen thousand pounds of tobacco, to be levied by the vestry of each parish respectively upon the citizens of that parish, and collected as other taxes; that no minister should preach without ordination by a Bishop in England; that any person not so ordained attempting to preach, publicly or privately, should be silenced by the Governor and Council, and if he persisted should be banished from the colony; that no other catechism should be taught but that contained in the Book of Common Prayer; that on every Sunday each person not necessarily confined at home, should attend the parish church of his own parish, under a penalty for failure of fifty pounds of tobacco; and that each non-conformist should pay twenty pounds sterling—about a hundred dollars—for each month's absence from the regular established Church of the parish in which he resided; and if absent a year, should be apprehended, and required to give security for his good behaviour, which, if he failed to do, he should be imprisoned until he conformed to the Church, or gave the security demanded.*

By these and other similar Ecclesiastical laws, the people of Virginia were governed up to the time of the American Revolution, if we except the brief period of Cromwell's Protectorate, during which the affairs of the Church were taken out of the custody of the Legislature, and placed in the hands of the Parishes; and the ameliorating influence of "The Act of Toleration," which never was published at length in the colony, and therefore to the masses of the people, was for many years wholly unknown.†

Under the government which we have now described, what could the Baptists of Virginia do? Was any movement looking towards a denominational organization possible? Apologists for the Episcopal Church in Virginia, such as Dr. Hawks and others, have told us that these and similar laws were inoperative, and remained in the Statute books "a dead letter." It is also intimated that persecutions did not commence until near the close of the colonial period,

* Journals of the Legislature, passim. Hening, &c., vols. 1, 2.
† Hening, &c., pref. vol. 1, p. 15.

when they were provoked by the agitations and insubordination of the Baptists. No man reveres more sincerely than I do the memory of the early colonists of Virginia. I would deal with their faults with all kindness. But to conceal the truth, even were it lawful, is both useless and impracticable. History speaks in a tone not to be suppressed, and she affirms in unmistakable language, that "persecutions for conscience" were rife in Virginia from the very beginning of its government. Who, for example, were those "inhabitants of Montserrat," a place in the West Indies, of whom the Jesuit White speaks in his "Pilgrims of Maryland," and of whom he incidentally says, under date of 1634, "They were driven from Virginia for their religious opinions." * Have we not already seen that four men, who had been soldiers of Cromwell, were hung, evidently for no other offence than their religious opinions? Was not the penalty of the law inflicted to the letter, as Hening informs us, upon a citizen in 1640, whose name he does not record? Did not Stevenson Reek suffer, in 1643, the most revolting severities for religious offences? He stood in the pillory two hours with a label on his back, paid a fine of fifty pounds, and was imprisoned at the pleasure of the Governor." † Were not the Congregational ministers, Thompson, Knolles, James, and Harrison—sent as Missionaries to Virginia by the General Court in Boston—banished in 1648 from the colony? and were not their congregation, though meeting only in private, violently broken up, dispersed, and some of them imprisoned during in-

* Annals of Annapolis, p. 23.   † Burke, vol. 2, p. 57.

definite periods? * And James Pyland, the member from Isle of Wight County, what was "his the said Pyland's blasphemous Catechism," for the issuing of which he was expelled in 1652 from the "House of Burgesses?" † Was not the member from Norfolk also expelled from the "House of Burgesses" in 1663, on a religious account? ‡ And upon what authority were Baptists in later years apprehended, imprisoned, fined, and tortured? Would to God these laws had remained "a dead letter on the Statute book." But alas! the sufferings and groans and blood of many a victim, clamoring in our ears, reveal on the part of the rulers of those times, not the soft forbearance claimed for them by partial and interested apologists, but a relentless cruelty, and deeds of misery and death!

Some of the laws enacted by the colonial government seem, as far as we can now understand them, to have been especially designed for the suppression of Baptist principles. The law of 1661–2, for example, was as follows:

"Whereas, many schismatical persons, out of their averseness to the orthodox established religion, or out of the new-fangled conceit of their own heretical inventions, do refuse to have their children baptized; Be it, therefore, enacted by the authority aforesaid, that all persons that in contempt of the divine sacrament of Baptism, shall refuse when they may carry their child [children] to a lawful minister of that county to

* Holmes' Annals, p. 289.–Savage's Winthrop, p. 334.
† Hening's Stat. at Large, vol. 1, pp. 374, 375.
‡ Hening ut Supra, vol. 2, p. 198.

have them baptized, shall be amerced two thousand pounds of tobacco; half to the informer; half to the public." *

Study this enactment. It is instructive. It might have embraced Quakers, some of whom are known to have been in the colony, but that it had special regard to Baptists no one can reasonably doubt. The preamble declares, that there were *many* persons in Virginia that refused to have their children baptized; that they did not neglect merely, but *refused* to have that ordinance administered to their little ones; and that their refusal was based upon *principle*, which the act pronounces to have been "averseness to the orthodox established religion," "or the new-fangled conceit of their own heretical inventions." These opposers of infant baptism were not infidels; they were not profane men; they were not people who were careless of their religious obligations; they were intelligent, thinking, conscientious Christians; such as the law pronounces stubborn *heretics*, pestilential *schismatics*, averse to Episcopacy, and led in their religion by *their own* heretical inventions. Plainly also they were not men of little consideration, since, in that case, legislative enactments regarding them would have been thought superfluous; but they were men of such character, and influence in society, as to threaten by their example, in the opinion of the Legislature, the safety of the established religion. The government, therefore, believed it necessary to interpose, and by fines and denunciations to overbear their consciences, and

* Hening's Stat. at Large, vol. 2, pp. 165, 166.

to compel their conformity to the Church of England.

The facts now before us show that, by the laws of the colony, any persons daring to teach the people doctrines or practices, other than those prescribed by the Church of England, were to be imprisoned until they should be reclaimed, or if they could not be reclaimed, sent to England for punishment; that every person in the colony, male and female, was obliged when called upon to go to the minister, and give a true statement of his or her faith; to attend the Episcopal service every Sabbath day; and to be present, and answer publicly, whenever the minister should " catechise; " that no minister not conformed to the Church of England, should, under the severest penalties, be permitted to teach or to preach, publicly or privately; that every colonist should pay his assessed proportion of the taxes for the support of the Episcopal Church; that no catechism should be taught but that contained in the book of Common Prayer; that any person not conforming to the Church, absence from the services of which was to be the proof, was to pay a fine of a hundred dollars a month, and if not reclaimed within twelve months, was to be imprisoned until he did conform, and give the Church security that he would maintain his conformity; and every one was compelled by fines to have his children baptized. These, and similar laws, the Governor, the Council of State, and the ministers of religion, all ready enough to it, were enjoined to execute; and to make the punishments sure, informers were suborned by the payment to them of half the fines imposed upon offenders.

Under the operation of such laws; watched by vigilant enemies on every side; no minister, known to be such, permitted to reside in the colony, is it surprising that in Virginia no Baptist churches were organized, and no gospel ordinances administered? Still, though overborne and suppressed for a hundred years, Baptist principles were "secure in their own immortality;" and were, even in Virginia, silently, unobtrusively, but effectually laying a foundation for subsequent glorious triumphs.

CHAPTER IV.

BAPTIST PRINCIPLES IN VIRGINIA FIRST EMBODIED IN VISIBLE CHURCHES.

Mistakes on the subject.   Act of Toleration.   Correspondence with English Baptists.   Nordin and White.   Constitution of a church at Burleigh, south of James River.   Other churches in its neighborhood organized.   Churches in Loudon, Berkeley, and other places in the northern part of the colony.   Loveall, Heaton, Garrard and other ministers.   Causes of Baptist impunity.   Philadelphia Association.

THE dreary night which had brooded so long in unbroken silence over Virginia began at last to recede. Approaching day was visible in the spiritual horizon. The Baptists of the colony shook off their slumbers, and awoke to cheerfulness and hope.   It is not known that any Baptist ministers were in the colony either as residents or visitors.   There were, however, men of intelligence, influence, and energy, who were not content to remain longer inactive.   The names and position of these men cannot now be known, but their noble deeds have become immortal.   We know only that they all resided on the south side of James River. After the necessary consultation, they decided to move together in the cause of Christ, which they did vigorously and successfully.   One, and another, and another Baptist Church sprang up in the colony, like so many camp fires upon the hills, whose light penetrated in all directions the surrounding gloom.

5

Very little attention has been given by Baptist writers to the circumstances under which Baptist principles in Virginia were first embodied in visible churches. The accounts of Pedobaptists, from which mainly the reading world have derived their impressions are singularly erroneous and distorted. The statements of Dr. Hawks in his "History of the Protestant Episcopal Church in Virginia," may be taken as an example. This learned gentleman tells his readers that the first *Baptist emigrants* to Virginia arrived in 1714; that no *churches* appeared until 1765, fifty-one years afterwards; that these churches sprang up in *Amelia* County; and that their preachers came from the North.* It is very well known by all who have taken the trouble to inquire, and as we shall presently see, that in 1765 there were in Virginia more than *fifty* Baptist churches; that in Amelia County Baptist principles did not at first prevail; and that their early preachers came, not from the North, but from England, and were sent out by Baptist churches in the city of London. These and other like falsifications of history arise, as is presumed, not so much from any wish on the part of the writers to misrepresent facts, as from their indisposition to seek the necessary information, and their general carelessness on the whole subject. Doubtless, they had somewhere read or heard such reports, and without examination recorded them as true. Whether, however, these misrepresentations were the results of ignorance, of carelessness, or of design, they ought long since to have

---

* Hist. Prot. Epis. Ch. in Va., pp. 120, 121.

been exposed and corrected. No candid or ingenuous Pedobaptist desires to be led astray by false history. Have Baptists had in their own ranks none who cared for the memory, or had sufficient courage to vindicate the honor of the fathers? Why then, up to this hour, have they remained uncontradicted and unrefuted? Which of all the numerous and able Baptist writers that our country has produced, has even reviewed any of these volumes of which we complain, or in any other manner sought to turn aside their injurious representations? Not one! On the contrary, while some have amused themselves with these fables, others have repeated them as true, and thus given them an authority with the masses which otherwise they never could have acquired.

"The Act of Toleration" was adopted by the British Parliament, during the first year of the reign of William and Mary. The colonial authorities earnestly maintained that this act was not operative in Virginia. Therefore, it was kept as much as possible from the knowledge of the people. In this construction several of the other colonies concurred. The court in New York, for example, as may be seen in the case of Rev. Mr. Mackamie, a Presbyterian minister, declared that it was inoperative in America!

The Act of Toleration, as it stands upon the English Statute book, is entitled "An Act for exempting their Majesties' Protestant subjects, dissenting from the Church of England, from penalties of certain laws." That it was not "operative" in the American colonies, was a monstrous pretension, needless now to be discussed. Strictly, however, if interpreted according to its terms, it could not extend to Baptists, either in Great Britain or America, since Baptists, although "subjects of their Majesties," and "dissenting from the Church of England" were not, never had been, and are not now Protestants. The government, however, of both countries, chose to place them in that category. The law, therefore, was evidently *designed* to embrace them, and that it did not was the mistake of those by whom it was framed. Baptists needed too much the indulgence, imperfect and humiliating as it was, which it offered, to explain or object. Although never published in Virginia, its existence was necessarily admitted, but always in an ambiguous manner. The facts in this case may be stated on account of their singularity.

The first acknowledgment in Virginia of the law in question occurred ten years after its adoption by the Mother Country, and then only as a proviso of "An Act entitled an Act for the more effectual suppressing of blasphemy, swearing, cursing, drunkenness, and Sabbath-breaking," adopted by the Legislature during its session of 1699. This is the relation in which it is introduced. That Act concludes as follows :—"Provided always, that if any person or persons, dissenting from the Church of England, being every way qualified according to an Act of Parliament made in the first year of our sovereign Lord, the king that now is, and the late Queen Mary of blessed memory, entitled 'An Act for exempting their Majesties' subjects, dissenting from the Church of England, from penalties of

certain laws,' shall resort and meet at any congregation or place of religious worship, permitted, and
allowed by the said Act of Parliament, once in two
months, that then the said penalties and forfeitures,
imposed by the Act [this act for the more effectual
suppressing of blasphemy, swearing, cursing, drunkenness, and Sabbath-breaking, as above, and] for refu-
sing to resort to their parish church or chapel as aforesaid, shall not be taken to extend to such person, or
persons." In this manner did the Legislature seek to
attach a disgrace to all who should attempt to avail
themselves of "The Act of Toleration." In the fifth
Revisal of the Laws of Virginia, which was made in
1705, in Act 30th the Law of Toleration is referred to
in terms still more slight and ambiguous. This was
"An Act for the suppression of vice." It appears
only by an allusion in a parenthesis. Those interested
were left to discover, as best they could, the privileges
to which by that Act they were entitled.*

Beverly, in his "History and Present State of Virginia," explains the provisions of the Law of Toleration. He says, "The people are generally of the
Church of England, which is the religion established
by law in the country, from which there are few dissenters. Yet liberty of conscience is given to all other
congregations *pretending* to *Christianity*, on condition
they submit to *all parish duties.*" † We ought not to
dismiss this subject without ascertaining to what
extent, and upon what conditions, as prescribed and

---

* Foote's Sketches of the Presbyterian Church in Virginia, pp. 48, 49.
† Edit. 1705, Book 4, Part. I chap. 7, p. 27.

regulated by "the Act of Toleration," liberty of conscience" was conceded to Protestants dissenting from the Church of England. This famous law demanded that all such Dissenters should pay their full proportion for the support of the parish ministers of the Establishment, after which they might support their own pastor, if they had one, and were able to do so; that they should receive marriage at the hands of the Episcopal minister, and in the parish church, no other being lawful or allowed to any one; that they should pay all parish rates for building and repairing the State Church meeting-houses, and for purchasing, repairing, and improving the glebes, and after they had done this, they might if they could, build meeting-houses of their own; that these conditions fulfilled, if they could obtain a license for a place as a house of worship, they might meet there and worship God; that if their minister could procure from the Government a license to preach at that place, he might preach there, but nowhere else; and that as many persons as could prove that they attended such preaching once in two months (by a subsequent amendment, once a month) they were on these conditions and to this extent, exempt from the pains and penalties denounced in previous laws against all those Protestants who could not conscientiously conform to "the constitution and canons, the doctrines and services, of the Church of England!" Such was toleration in *England*, and when at last it was admitted to be operative, such was toleration in *Virginia* under this statute of William and Mary! Such was the extent of "liberty of conscience" in the best and most liberal days of Episcopal rule in the colony.

These miserable and reluctant concessions were meager indeed; still they were an advancement in the direction of "Religious Freedom." They were, therefore, with all their humiliating conditions, accepted by the people, who were thereby emboldened, not only to express their religious sentiments freely, but also to carry them out in their public action as far as these provisions permitted. Now they could appear as they supposed, in their true character, without the risk of imprisonment, fines, and banishment from the country which contained all that was dear to them upon earth. The several denominations then existing in the colony, oppressed, persecuted, and scattered, naturally sought intercourse with those of their own faith. The Baptists especially were encouraged to undertake such measures as seemed to them best, looking to the organization in Virginia of churches upon the apostolic model.

Another consideration had especial influence with them in some quarters. In Isle of Wight, Surry, and other South-eastern counties, large numbers of persons cherishing Baptist sentiments, found themselves together. This is the region from which, in previous years, as we have before seen, upon the authority of Historical Sketches, by Morgan Edwards, numerous families, to escape the heartless oppressions of the State Church, had emigrated to North Carolina. Refering to the subject, Dr. Benedict says:—"William Sojourner, a most excellent man, and useful minister,

removed with many of his brethren from Burleigh, in
Virginia, and settled on Kehuki Creek, in the county
of Halifax, and the same year planted the church in
that place." He further says:—"Most of the first
Baptist churches in North Carolina are said to have
emigrated from Burleigh in Virginia." *

This oppression and exodus may be accounted for
perhaps, by the fact, that in that part of the colony were
erected many large and elegant "colonial churches,"
some of which were the most expensive and magnificent buildings of the kind then in America. The
ruins of these buildings, and especially of one now in
the woods near Smithfield, in Isle of Wight, even at
this day excite the amazement of all who visit them.
To erect these "splendid structures," which doubtless
pleased the taste of some clergymen, younger sons of
noble families in England, all the people, and Baptists as well as others, were obliged to pay heavily,
and worship in them afterwards. They resolved not
to do this, and as the only alternative, left the colony.
Many, however, still remained, who having no ministers to suggest measures, or to lead the way, assembled
of their own accord to advise with each other as to
what ought to be done to supply their spiritual wants.
These men were not, as Dr. Hawks asserts, a company
of emigrants from England, but residents of the country, of long and influential standing. After frequent
and prayerful consultations they decided to address a
joint communication, not to their friends in the northern colonies, but to their friends in England, and

* History of the Baptists, vol. 2, p. 97.

especially in the city of London, where at that time Baptist churches abounded, having emerged from the oppressions under which until the administration of Cromwell, they had unceasingly labored. Speaking of these times, Mr. Davis, in his "History of the Welsh Baptists," * says, "God gave the Baptists a respite from persecution, and they were allowed to meet together, and to devise plans for the advancement of the Redeemer's Kingdom. As early as 1653, they were emboldened to meet in an Association at Abergavenny, Wales, where missionary arrangements, designed to be of a permanent character, were inaugurated." The reign of the second Charles, however, suspended all their public efforts, and during the bitter persecutions which followed, many of their ministers and leading members either fled from the country or died in prison."

The first year of the reign of William and Mary was, as we have seen, rendered memorable by the adoption of the Act of Toleration. The Baptists were again somewhat relieved, and in 1689 met in a great Association in the city of London. One hundred and seven churches, as appears from Rippon's Register,† were present by their messengers. The proceedings of each day are briefly recorded. Here they renewed their missionary organization, and adopted measures for more systematic and effectual labors. This was the body addressed by the citizens of Virginia, and which they earnestly solicited to send them Baptist ministers for their instruction and guidance. Whether the correspondence, official and private, then had between

* Pp. 85, et seq.   † Passim.

these parties, can now be found, is perhaps questionable. If it can be brought to light,—and it is hoped
that an earnest effort will be made for its discovery,—
it will throw a flood of light on the history of "The
Early Baptists of Virginia." This correspondence
occurred in 1713. The solicitations of the Virginians
were kindly entertained by their friends in the British
metropolis, and in May 1714, they ordained two
of their own number, Robert Nordin, and Thomas
White, and sent them as missionaries to the colony.
Mr. White died on the passage hither, and was buried
at sea. Mr. Nordin in due time arrived, and commenced his labors. These ministers were soon after
followed by others, sent out and sustained by the same
churches in London and its neighborhood, among
whom, as faithful laborers in South Eastern Virginia,
the names of Jones, of Mintz, and of others, are still
familiar. All these gentlemen were received by the
people here, with the warmest affection and confidence,
and having complied with the conditions of the Act of
Toleration, preached and baptized, not only without
molestation from the colonial authorities, but with the
most gratifying success. Their labors resulted in the
organization, during the first year of their residence,
1715, of a church at Burleigh, in Isle of Wight
County, which has since taken the name—less classical
indeed, but also less exposed to popular prejudice—
of Mill Swamp. Another church was soon afterwards
constituted at Brandon, in Surry County, believed to be
that now known as Otter Dams. From this time
Baptist churches sprang up rapidly in all the southern

and lower counties in the colony. These were the first churches, embodying Baptist principles, that were planted in Virginia.

Not long after these events, our attention is attracted by others of a like character, in the *northern* part of the colony. Previous to 1743, numerous Baptists were found residing in Loudon, Berkeley, and contiguous counties. A large and flourishing settlement had been made by the Welsh, in Pennsylvania, which already contained several Baptist churches. At the solicitation of these isolated Christians in Virginia, they were visited by Messrs. Loveall, Heaton, Garrard, and others, ministers from Pennsylvania, who preached and instructed the people faithfully and successfully. Here also, as in the South, churches immediately sprang up. The first was Opecon, the next Mill Creek, then Ketocton, and then numerous others. From these two centres, churches soon extended themselves throughout the whole Virginia colony.

From a very early period Baptist churches in the old world had been, for special purposes, accustomed to form themselves into Associations. None of these Associations were ever clothed with any power whatever to govern the churches of which they were composed. Our Lord Jesus Christ, the Head of all the churches, has delegated to each church full powers for its own government, but nothing more. Delegated power cannot be redelegated by those upon whom it is conferred, without the consent of the original authority. No such consent, for any purpose whatever, is found in the word of God. Churches cannot, therefore, divest themselves of the right of self-government. It is inalienable. They cannot bestow it upon associations, nor upon any other body of churches, upon clergymen, or any synod, convention, or conference outside of themselves. For these reasons, and also because Associations are bodies unknown to the Scriptures, they never can in any manner govern the churches or control their government. They were instituted by the Fathers as bodies in which the messengers of the churches might annually meet, make known to each other their progress, condition, and wants; give to each other such advice and assistance as should be necessary or practicable; and agree upon judicious measures to extend the preaching of the gospel into destitute places, and assist feeble churches, wherever such places and churches were found. Such were the Association of which we have spoken, at Abergavenny, in Wales, in the time of Cromwell, and the Association in London, in the time of William III, that sent missionaries to the Virginia colony. Such an Association had already been formed in Pennsylvania, then and now known as the Philadelphia Association. With this body, all the churches in Virginia united, and they derived from this membership, while it continued, many and very great advantages, since they were constantly favored with its advice and assistance, and visited by its ministers, and especially by James Miller, David Thomas, and John Gano, who labored among them with extraordinary success.

The impunity with which the Baptists now preached and organized churches, arose from several co-opera-

ting causes. None of the laws against dissenters, to
which in former chapters we have referred at large,
had been repealed, but they had been essentially modified in their practical operation, by the "Statute of
Toleration," and the opinion began very generally to
prevail, that if citizens paid their tithes and other dues
for the support of the Established Church; were otherwise good and loyal subjects of the king of England;
did not by their religious services injure or disturb
their neighbors; and had the prescribed government
licenses, they might be suffered to worship God in
their own way, without molestation. And further, the
excessive bigotry which had been imported from the
Old World, and which so long ran rampant in the
colony, had by its very extravagance overthrown itself.
A reaction had now fairly set in, the power of which
could not be successfully resisted. Therefore, if Baptists kept themselves within ordinary bounds, not much
inclination existed to inquire whether they were in all
respects conformed to the intolerant statutes of the Legislature. And still further. At the time of which
we now write, the ministry and most of the membership of the State Church had fallen into a state of almost utter demoralization. They revelled in wealth
and luxury; they were careful only of their revenues
and their pleasures; and secure in their own power
and position, they cared little for the spiritual condition
or wants of the masses of the people. They were the
lords of the land, beyond the reach of ordinary con-
tingencies; their contempt for the Baptists did not permit them to inquire much into their proceedings; and

6

therefore they gave them very little disturbance. These causes taken together exerted an extraordinary power. They were an effectual shield against the uplifted hand of persecution and oppression. The grand cause, however, was the blessing of God. "The time to favor Zion, yea the set time, had come." The truth of the gospel had struck its roots deeply into the mental soil of the people. Church after church noiselessly shone forth, like the stars in an evening sky ; and sparkling as so many gems in the Virginia firmament, which they were destined to fill ere long with celestial radiance and beauty.

CHAPTER V.

PROGRESS OF BAPTIST PRINCIPLES IN VIRGINIA.

Arrival and ministry of Stearns and Marshall. Prevalence of revival. Ministers among the converts. Multiplication of churches. Organization of associations. The Kehuki. The Charleston. The Sandy Creek. The Ketocton. The General Association of Virginia.

THE arrival of Shubael Stearns inaugurated a new era in the history of "The Early Baptists of Virginia." That gentleman was born and educated in the city of Boston; was "a *Minister* of the Established Order" of Massachusetts; had been compelled from principle to become a Baptist; had been baptized and ordained in his native city; and, persecuted and harassed at home, had wandered to the South in hopes of greater usefulness, bringing with him his little helpless family. He had no place especially in view. He reached at length the Virginia colony, where he determined to rest at least for a season. Accordingly he took up his residence at Cacapon, in Hampshire County, where with great earnestness and many anxieties, he commenced modestly to preach the gospel to the people. Soon after the settlement of Mr. Stearns, he was joined by his brother-in-law, Daniel Marshall, and his family. Mr. Marshall was a Presbyterian minister, born and educated in Windsor, Connecticut. He had, following the example of Elliott, devoted himself to the work of a missionary among the Indians. In that capacity, he had labored for several years with a tribe on the Susquehanna river, in Pennsylvania. War, however, broke out between that tribe and the colony of Maryland, and instant confusion and destruction were all around him. Despairing of any further benefit to the Indians, he retired in deep sorrow from the scene of his sacrifices and toils. Naturally he bent his steps towards the contiguous residence of his relatives in Virginia, of which fortunately he had received some information. Meantime, studying carefully the word of God, and isolated from those influences that might have turned aside his conclusions, Mr. Marshall had also become a convert to the Baptist faith. Without unnecessary delay, he was baptized, ordained as a Baptist minister, and with all his great abilities and extraordinary zeal, entered with his brother-in-law upon the work of preaching the gospel to the Virginians.

In all these events the directing hand of God soon became unmistakably apparent. The activity and laborious exertions upon which these two men now entered, were in modern times wholly unprecedented. They did not confine their labors to the vicinity of their residences, but visited other places, and were soon traveling and preaching throughout the whole length and breadth of the colony. Everywhere they found on the part of the people a warm reception. The fields were "white unto the harvest." God was in his own truth. One universal impulse appeared to pervade the minds of all classes. Hungering for the bread of life, they came together in vast multitudes. Surprising success everywhere attended their ministry. Very large numbers were converted and baptized.

Churches sprang up by scores, all of which prospered, and multiplied, and rejoiced. The waves from the south of the colony, met those from the north. The whole land resounded with songs of gratitude and thanksgiving.

Among the converts, were men of all ranks and positions in society. The high and the low, the rich and the poor, the free and the bond, all met in their churches upon the gospel level, where every one gladly took such part as he was able in the services. Soon not a few manifested superior qualifications for the ministry, and affectionately encouraged by their brethren, entered enthusiastically upon the work. The ranks of the messengers of salvation were daily swelling. Higher and still higher the tide continued to rise. The mingled perseverance and energy with which they all, ministers and people, continued in the work, were amazing, and the rapidity with which the gospel was transmitted from neighborhood to neighborhood may be not unfitly described in the language with which Æschylus depicts the progress of the beacon fires that announced the fall of Troy :—

> "From watch to watch it leaped, that light,
> As a rider rode the flame."

The people seem to have lost sight almost entirely of the parish churches, and ministers of the established religion, thinly scattered through the country. Their services were attended by a few families only, of high aristocratic pretensions, whose pride of position demanded "a religion fit for gentlemen." Few or no Presbyterians or Congregationalists were then in Virginia; the Methodists had not commenced their career in this country; and the field was left to the almost exclusive occupancy of the Baptists. Under their vigorous cultivation, it bloomed like the garden of God. "The wilderness and the solitary place were glad for them, and the desert rejoiced and blossomed as the rose. It blossomed abundantly, and rejoiced even with joy and singing. The glory of Lebanon was given unto them; the excellency of Carmel and Sharon. They saw the glory of the Lord; and the excellency of our God."

The Baptists of both the Carolinas had preceded in their movements those of Virginia. The governments of these colonies were much less bigoted and intolerant, and their people were, therefore, more free. In them both, therefore, were early found numerous and flourishing churches. Those in the eastern part of North Carolina, finding attendance upon the sessions of the Philadelphia Association, on account of the great distance, extremely inconvenient, indeed almost impracticable, met in Convention some time previous to 1750, and organized upon the parent model the Kehuki Association, which embraced all those churches in Virginia, south of the James River, from the Appomattox to the sea. The previous affinity of the Baptists in these two sections of country, has been explained in a former chapter.* Influenced by the same considerations the churches in South Carolina, including some in southern North Carolina, assembled

* Vide, ch. 2.

in 1751, and organized the Charleston Association, a body since distinguished for its extraordinary learning, energy, and usefulness. The fourth Association in the order of time formed among the Baptists of North America, was the Sandy Creek, organized in 1758, and composed of the churches in the upper portion of North Carolina, with those in the contiguous portion of Virginia, south of James River, and west of the Appomattox. The whole of the churches in Virginia between the James River and the Potomac—and they had now become very numerous—still retained their connection with the Philadelphia Association. Feeling the same inconveniences with the other churches further south, and moved by their example, they met in Convention, and organized the Ketocton Association. All these associations were formed with the advice and approval of the parent body. They covered an area of three colonies. Between them all, mother and daughter, scattered from the Hudson to the Savannah River, the most perfect affection and harmony of intercourse prevailed. These organizations did much for the time to consolidate the denomination, and to accelerate its progress.

The State Church and ministry of Virginia, vexed with the extraordinary progress of the Baptists, and mortified at finding themselves forsaken by their congregations, thousands of whom had professed religion, and united with their churches, awoke as from a dream. They had entrenched themselves carefully, and imagined that no danger could approach them. Suddenly they found themselves undermined, and

almost wholly subverted.   Their former contempt now
changed to indignation, and they assumed an attitude
of hostility.   Unmistakable indications appeared that
they would soon commence in earnest the work of persecution, and if possible overwhelm the Baptist
churches and their cause.   Already the established
ministry were preaching earnestly and persistently a
crusade against them, and calling loudly upon the
colonial authorities to execute rigorously the laws
against dissenters.   Against the injuries likely to result from this cause, the Baptists believed it necessary
that they should adopt some measures, which in the
judgment of the wise and prudent might be thought
the most effectual.

The whole country, they saw evidently, was rapidly
approaching a momentous political crisis, the probable
results of which filled them with mingled apprehension
and hope.   An armed collision with the Mother
Country seemed almost inevitable.   Should that event
occur, and the rebel colonies be subdued and brought
back under the English yoke, the prospects of the
Baptists in this country would be dark indeed.   All
their glorious prosperity would be overthrown, their
churches crushed, and the whole cause thrown back
into the position which it occupied a hundred years
before.   The thought that such a calamity might over-
take them was horrible.   On the other hand, indistinct
prospects appeared to their minds, that should a revolution occur, and should the colonies achieve their
freedom and secure the organization of a new government, they might in the providence of God be able,

not only to free themselves from the tyranny and oppression of the State Church, but also to engraft " Religious Liberty," in the legitimate Baptist sense, in the laws of Virginia at least, and perhaps in the laws of the whole country. As citizens, and as men, they had the same interests at stake with all others. But beyond these, as Christians, they looked to infinitely higher considerations. In their estimation, nearly all that is precious in the gospel of Christ, in its bearing upon the extension of truth in this world, and the preparation of the soul for salvation in the world to come, was now to be gained effectually, or lost for perhaps yet many a slow and weary century. To the Baptists, all these considerations seemed plainly involved in the approaching struggle.

By what means could the ministry and churches in Virginia best concentrate all their energies, and bring them to bear upon these momentous interests, so as to control and direct them as effectually as possible? These questions were submitted to the churches, and discussed, publicly and privately, with great anxiety and earnestness. At their sessions in 1770, it was unanimously determined to meet in Convention and organize a new Association in Virginia, to the supervision and direction of which all these interests, and nothing else, should be especially committed. This proposed combination, as will be seen, was unique and unprecedented. Exactly such another perhaps never existed before, and never has existed since. It was, however, timely, judicious, prompt, energetic; and, notwithstanding some dangerous aberrations, achieved results which ought to embalm its memory in the grateful heart, not only of every Christian, but also of every freeman in America.

The Convention assembled according to appointment, on the second Saturday in May, 1771, at Craig's, in Orange County. Large numbers were in attendance. A constitution was adopted, which pledged it never to attempt to exercise any authority over the churches, legislative, judicial, or executive, but to give itself exclusively to the interest confided by them to its care. It was then solemnly constituted and organized by prayer, under the name of " The General Association of Virginia." * The necessary Officers, Board, and Commissions were appointed, and received special instructions, and then "The General Association" adjourned to its next annual meeting. Thus originated that remarkable body, whose talents, energy, and fidelity have never been surpassed, and whose proceedings will occupy a large space in some of our succeeding chapters.

* Semple's History of the Virginia Baptists, p. 4, et seq.

CHAPTER VI.

CAUSES OF BAPTIST SUCCESS IN VIRGINIA.

Character of the people. Demoralization of the State Church. Persecutions of the Baptists. Their manner of preaching.

WE now return, and will review as carefully as practicable the causes which led to the extraordinary success with which "The Early Baptists of Virginia" were favored. The grand cause was undoubtedly the blessing of God upon his own truth. This truth they loved, embraced, adorned, and taught; and under such circumstances he will sooner or later make it triumphant. There were, however, secondary causes, providential circumstances and events, appropriate instrumentalities, all of which combined to strengthen and facilitate their cause. One of these is found in *the peculiar character of the people of Virginia.*

The citizens of this colony were isolated almost completely from the great world in which they lived. Widely scattered in their deep forests, among their beautiful hills, and upon their broad and fertile plains, their minds naturally assumed a bold and vigorous character. Savage enemies prowled around them on every side. To preserve their families and friends from their murderous incursions, every man was compelled to plan and execute his own method of defence. Their domestic and pecuniary affairs, they were obliged to conduct with very little counsel from others. In a word, they were obliged on all subjects to think for themselves. They acquired, in consequence, habits of self-reliance, which extended themselves into every department of life, to temporal things and to spiritual things, to the things of this world and of the world to come. This disposition once formed can never afterwards be repressed. A free and independent mind will think and act freely. It may be harassed and coerced, but it cannot be subdued. The yeomanry of Virginia were, therefore, not the men to be overawed by rulers or carried away by those prejudices or perverted principles that flow out from cities and rich and populous neighborhoods. With the Bible in their hands, and little else in the form of literature, and accustomed to think and act independently, they heard impartially the preaching of the Baptists, and were prepared to weigh diligently and candidly their teachings. They saw that these teachings embraced truly the gospel of our Lord Jesus Christ. They gave them, therefore, their full and hearty assent.

Another cause of the great success of " The Early Baptists of Virginia " is to be sought in *the character of the then established religion* of the colony.

The trammels of an established religion, even when in its doctrines and forms it is comparatively unobjectionable, are not usually relished by the masses of the people, and especially by those who read for themselves the word of God and are accustomed to mental freedom. To them, such a religion seems designed rather for courtly form and ceremony, or to subserve political purposes, than to promote the salvation and sanctification of the soul. Especially are they not likely to be hearty in the payment of the heavy taxes assessed by the government for its support. But when that religion has, on whatever account, ceased to command their respect, and other doctrines, forms, and teachers seem to them more consonant with the word of God, then they look upon it with feelings of repulsion, and obedience is secured only by a power which compels it. Precisely such a state of things as this now existed in Virginia. The people had ceased to feel any special reverence for the Church, and of its bonds and its burdens they had become heartily tired. Nor was this all. With her arrogant pretensions, her persecuting spirit, and her general demoralization, they had become thoroughly disgusted. They were, therefore, willing to hear the Baptists, and not disinclined to embrace and practice their principles.

The moral condition of "The Protestant Episcopal Church in Virginia,"—then established by law,—at the time of which we write, ought to be more fully presented. Dr. Semple, referring to that period, remarks:—"The loose and immoral deportment of her clergy was such, that the people were left almost entirely destitute of even the shadow of religion. They had, indeed, some of the forms of worship, but the essential principles of Christianity were not only not understood among them, but by many were never heard of."* Dr. Hawks himself is not less explicit than Dr. Semple. Quoting from Hammond, he says:—"They could babble in a pulpit, roar in a tavern, exact from

* Hist. of Va. Bapt., pp. 25, 26.

7

their parishioners, and rather by their dissoluteness destroy than feed the flock."* In another place, Dr. Hawks says, Many of the clergy "were unfit for their duties." He adds: "The precariousness of the tenure by which they held their livings, contributed also not a little to beget in them a spirit of indifference to the discharge of their duties; and to complete the list of unpropitious circumstances, the irregularities and crimes of an unworthy clergyman could not be visited effectually with the severities of ecclesiastical censure."† So scandalous did these evils at length become, that a remedy was attempted by the Legislature of the Commonwealth. An extract from the law of 1776 will sufficiently explain the facts involved. It is as follows: "Be it further enacted by this Grand Assembly, and by the authority thereof, that such ministers as shall become notoriously scandalous by drunkenness, swearing, fornication, or other heinous and crying sins, and shall thereof be lawfully convicted, shall, for every such their heinous crime and wickedness,"—and the act proceeds to prescribe some petty and inconsiderable penalties.‡

This is a terribly revolting picture of clerical morals and manners. It is not to be presumed that all were of this character. Doubtless there were good men among them. What proportion of them were drunken debauchees may be readily imagined. They remained unrebuked, since the Church possessed no power—if it

---

* Hist. Prot. Ep. Ch. in Va., p. 65.
† Hist. Prot. Ep. Ch. in Va., p. 89.
‡ Hening's Stat. at Large, Vol. II., p. 384.

had the inclination—to administer censure. The Legislature, therefore, undertook, by statute, to do the work of discipline. So far as appears, all these enactments remained nugatory. "Their heinous crimes and wickedness" went on unchecked. Is it surprising that for such a ministry and church the people should feel no reverence, and warmly oppose the taxes they were called upon to pay for their support?

Another source of dissatisfaction with the church and ministry of the Establishment arose. The rebellion broke out against the British government. *Large numbers of the clergy at once assumed a position on the side of England, and against the liberty of the colony.* They brought the subject into their pulpits; they denounced the people as insurrectionists and traitors; and commanded them to abandon their rebellion, and submit, without further resistance, to their legitimate rulers. So offensive were the sermons of some of them, that the citizens felt themselves insufferably outraged. On one occasion at least, a clergyman, after a Sunday's vaporing in the pulpit, was seized by his congregation, carried into a neighboring forest, fastened to a tree, and there received thirty-nine lashes vigorously administered. Another to avoid a like fate, carried his pistols into the pulpit, and laying them by the side of his prayer-book, in the presence of the assembly, told his congregation that he should proceed with the service; that England had a right to govern them; that he should read all the prayers for the king, the Royal family, and the government; that in his sermon he should say what he pleased; and that he would shoot any man and every man who at-tempted to restrain him." Referring to these two ex-amples, Dr. Hawks, an Episcopalian writer of our own day, does not disapprove the conduct of the ministers. The punishment inflicted in the former case, he denounces as insult and persecution, and of the latter he says: "Such firmness was not without its effect; the resolute minister was never interrupted; his house became the refuge of many of his persecuted brethren [tories]; and one of the surest places of safety."* Not many of the clergy, however, were so intrepid. The fearful and faint-hearted, therefore, fled with all practicable haste. Few of them had any sympathy with the spirit or movements of the Ameri-can people.

Earnestly apologizing for these clerical renegades and tories, Dr. Hawks further says: " The clergy were generally friends of the Mother Country." " Admit the fact that the view which they entertained was erroneous, still it might have been, and was in many cases, a very honest error." " The question as to the proper course to be pursued, was one on which honest and intelligent men might differ." " Before, therefore, we condemn all who, in the perilous struggle, took part with the Mother Country, we should place ourselves in imagination in their situation, and it may serve to temper the harshness of our judgment." "But the error was not confined to the clergy. A portion of the laity adopted their opinions; it was however very small, for the mass of the population in Virginia was

---

* Hist. Prot. Epis. Ch. in Va., pp. 145, 146, 147.

opposed to England; and this rendered the situation of the clergy only the more disagreeable."* It is useless to discuss the question with Dr. Hawks, whether the Episcopal clergy of that day, whom he himself characterizes as being so depraved in morals; and who were by a law of the "Grand Assembly," accused as drunkards, swearers, and fornicators, had not in their own opinion very good reasons for being the enemies of Virginia liberty; whether in their toryism they were not very honest, and very conscientious; whether they were not the only enemies in the Church to American freedom; and whether the patriotism of the masses did not render their position very disagreeable. It is enough to know that they adhered to the foe, and were the enemies of the people. The citizens were fighting for their country; on every battle-field they were pouring out their blood like water; the cry of Patrick Henry was echoed by every patriot, "Give me liberty, or give me death;" and all were in the midst of the deep and desperate struggle for existence. What then must have been the feelings with which they beheld their pastors in league with their enemies and destroyers. Their indignation must have been boundless. They cast them off with inexpressible scorn.

To whom, now, were they most likely to look for spiritual instruction, and guidance? Not with unwavering confidence to the Presbyterian ministry and church, since they, as such, manifested, as we shall hereafter see, especial prudence, and carefully main-

* Hist. Prot. Ep. Ch. &c., pp. 135. 136.

tained only such grounds as would afford them an opportunity of easy retreat, in case of danger, to their original political position; or, if the colonies should succeed, to join in their triumphs; and besides, they were very few in numbers. Not to the Methodists, since they at that time claimed to be part and parcel of the Established Church, but purified from its moral pollutions. They did not, as we shall see, conceal the fact, that they were unmitigated tories. Public confidence turned affectionately and confidingly to the Baptists. As patriots, they were well known to be above reproach. Not a Baptist could be found in Virginia, minister or layman, who did not espouse, and at every sacrifice and to the last extremity defend, the cause of liberty. They were also, at that period, well known as eminently prayerful and devoted Christians. The people heard their fervid discourse and witnessed their earnest piety with delight. When the love of Christ was shed abroad in their hearts, then they gladly united by thousands with the Baptist churches.

The *measures adopted* by the *colonial rulers* to suppress Baptist principles, *became a cause of their extraordinary success* in Virginia.

In every age of the Church the persecutions it has waged have been its deep dishonor. No State church has ever been known that has abstained from persecution. In this shame, that of Virginia had its full share. The progress of the Baptists was to the clergy and governing authorities, exceedingly offensive. The magistrates commenced to annoy the people, and especially the ministers, in every practicable way. They sought, as we have seen, to set aside the " Law of Toleration;" old and obsolete laws were hunted up and revived; and every effort was made for their enforcement. Assessments were made with renewed diligence; fines were imposed and collected in all possible cases; assemblages were assailed and violently dispersed; and pastors and ministers and private members of the churches were arrested, thrown into prison, dragged before the courts, insulted, brow-beaten, and ignominiously punished. All this and more is confessed by their own best writers. In his elaborate History of the Protestant Episcopal Church in Virginia, Dr. Hawks, himself says:—" No Dissenters in Virginia experienced for the time, harsher treatment than did the Baptists. They were beaten and imprisoned, and cruelty taxed its ingenuity to devise new modes of punishment and annoyance. The usual consequences followed; persecution made friends for its victims; and the men who were not permitted to speak in public found willing auditors in the sympathizing crowds who gathered around the prisons to hear them preach from the grated windows. It is not," he adds, "improbable that this very opposition imparted strength in another mode, inasmuch as it at length furnished the Baptists with common ground on which to make resistance." *

Dr. Hawks was not mistaken as to the results of this shameful persecution of the Baptists. The sympathies of the people were with them; crowds flocked

---

* History, &c., p. 121.

daily about their prisons; and the sermons they addressed to them from the grated windows, had an effect ten times greater than if they had been preached from the pulpit. The truth of this remark was illustrated by various examples; it was seen during the imprisonment of Waller, Craig, and others in Fredericksburg; of Waller, Greenwood, and their associates at Middlesex Court House; of Craig, Burruss, and others at Caroline Court House; and in the cases of those ministers who were incarcerated in the jails of Orange, Culpepper, Fauquier, Loudon, Chesterfield, and of various other counties. A venerable gentleman,* recently gone to his rest, some years ago said to his friend:—"I often heard, in my youth, the Baptist ministers preach from the windows of the Jail at Chesterfield Court House. The effects were sometimes most extraordinary. On one occasion Webber was preaching; the heavy iron gratings partially concealed him; his appeals were most touching. A man that I did not know, came up and stood by my side. In a few minutes this man began to tremble violently; presently he fell upon his knees, and then upon his face; and there he lay during the service, praying audibly and agonizingly to God for mercy and salvation through Jesus Christ." This, he added, "was no unusual occurrence. Scores and fifties were often at the same time similarly exercised." Eleazer Clay, Sheriff of the county, the uncle and guardian of the distinguished statesman, Henry Clay, with reference to those who had professed religion at Chesterfield Jail, writes

* Edward Bass, Esq.

thus to his friend, Rev. John Williams, of Amelia County :—

"We wish you to come down and baptize those who are now waiting for an opportunity. The Lord is now carrying on a glorious work in our county. The preaching at the prison is not attended in vain, for we hope that several are converted, while others are under great distress, and are made to cry out, ' What shall we do to be saved.'" *

The proceedings in all the other counties where Baptist ministers were imprisoned were substantially the same with those in Chesterfield. From these, as so many centres, the excitement extended itself throughout the whole country, and while it produced intense indignation against the clergy and magistrates, added immensely to the popularity and success of the Baptists of Virginia.

The consonance between the doctrines held by Baptists in every age and country on political subjects, and the *spirit of liberty* which had now taken full possession of the Virginia heart, was another cause of the extraordinary success of the Baptists in that commonwealth.

What these doctrines are, has been summarily stated. Their full concession by the governing powers was demanded. Mere toleration, in its ordinary sense, did not satisfy them. Indeed they held it to be wholly inadmissible, since it concedes the right of the government, which they deny, to interfere in the religion of its citizens. These principles were constantly pro-

---

* Taylor's Lives of Virginia Baptist Ministers, pp. 203, 204, First Edit.

claimed by "The Early Baptists of Virginia" in public and in private, from the prisons and from the pulpits of the colony, and declared by such men as Waller, Harriss, Craig, Stearns, Greenwood, Thomas, Webber, Marshall, Burruss, and their compeers—men who in social position, intelligence, wealth, and general respectability, were in no way below, and in piety infinitely above, their assailants and persecutors. By Episcopalians, and Methodists, and, to some extent, by Presbyterians, they were denounced as pestilential heresies, disorganizing doctrines, whose prevalence was always to be deplored, and whose influence was, by all practicable methods, and at the earliest moment, to be suppressed. To their importance and intrinsic value, the progress of events had at last opened the eyes of the people. They now saw plainly that no State that does not fully embrace them ever can be really free. The time of their triumph had come. The masses received them as propounded by the ministers of religion, and ranged themselves by thousands on the side of the Baptists.

To *the peculiar character of the preaching* of those times, however, more than to any other one cause, is to be ascribed the extraordinary success of the early Baptists of Virginia.

Practically the people had up to this time been almost without a preached gospel. The Baptist ministry arose, rapidly multiplied, and soon filled the country. Never was a body of ministers more completely adapted to the people for whom they labored, and the times in which they lived. They had, as we shall hereafter see, controversies among themselves, but these did not seriously retard their work, much as has been said to the contrary by their assailants, and even by their friends. They were on subjects on which good and learned men have in no age found themselves able to harmonize entirely. Their differences were, however, always discussed with prayerfulness, brotherly love, and Christian courtesy, and, therefore, soon happily terminated. Subsequent years exhibited less of these characteristics. Still it is true that no denomination that has existed through so many ages, and of numbers so great, has preserved a more perfect unanimity, or fallen into fewer great and incurable divisions than the Baptist. These facts are well known to every man who is familiar with Ecclesiastical History.

By far the greater portion of the Baptist ministers of that period, came from the masses of the people to whom they preached, and with whose character, circumstances, peculiarities, and wants they were, therefore, intimately familiar. They sympathized with them fully, and in all respects. They consequently knew how to form and direct their discourses, so as to produce the best results. They were all remarkable for cheerful gravity, earnest and fervent piety, and a deportment strikingly exemplary. No others were tolerated by the churches, who exercised in that day over ministers as well as private members the strictest discipline. No worldly emolument, honor, ease, or power tempted any of them to enter the pulpit. On the contrary, they were deterred from it by the prospect of almost certain poverty, a life of laborious toil, and constant persecutions and annoyances. Nothing could impel them, therefore, to this sacred work, but the love of Christ and an overwhelming desire for the happiness and salvation of men. They lived in the presence of God—prayer and intercourse with him occupied them incessantly; their souls were imbued with the spirit of Christ; they loved the souls of men; their conversation in society was eminently spiritual; and they readily imparted to their associates and hearers the feelings by which they were themselves actuated.

On their days of meeting, and at all their casual appointments for preaching, their congregations always assembled early, and seating themselves as they arrived, they invariably occupied the time until the services commenced in singing the songs of Zion, which were often mingled with prayer, somewhat in the form of the prayer-meetings of the present day. These songs were numerous; not always composed in the highest style of poetry, but invariably eminently devotional; they generally had choruses attached; the tunes were for the most part easy and somewhat rapid; they were readily committed to memory; and the whole congregation joined in them most heartily; so that often when the minister arose to speak the whole assembly was all glowing with the warmest feelings of devotion, and eminently prepared to hear with benefit his heavenly message. So delighted were the people with these exercises, that whenever they met at each other's houses they occupied themselves in a similar manner.

The sermons of the ministers, however learned or unlearned, were nearly all constructed upon the same model. That model embraced invariably the grand leading truths of the gospel. With great clearness and force, they first presented the lost condition of man by nature, the innate depravity of the human heart, and the impossibility of deliverance from spiritual death by the law, by gospel ordinances, or by any other acts of mere human obedience. They next depicted vividly the way of salvation through our Lord Jesus Christ, with all its gracious characteristics, bearings, and relations. Then followed an exposition of the manner in which the righteousness and merits of the Redeemer are personally applied, in the case of each believer, by the Holy Spirit of God, and of the nature and effects of "repentance towards God, and faith towards our Lord Jesus Christ." They now recounted some of the mental phenomena generally attendant upon true spiritual regeneration, with the temptations, trials, and encouragements characteristic of genuine Christian experience. They closed with an earnest appeal to Christians, suitably to adorn their holy profession, and to sinners, to repent, believe, and be saved. The style, manner, and elocution of their sermons varied, of course, as did the endowments of the preachers, but the grand truths they uttered were always the same. The minds of the people were kept constantly and intensely fixed upon these great principles. The results were most happy. Multitudes heard, believed, obeyed, and rejoiced.

These mainly, under God, were the causes which gave the Early Baptists of Virginia their extraordinary success; the independent character of the people; the demoralized condition of the State Church and minis-

8

try ; the measures they adopted to crush and destroy them ; the consonance between Baptist principles on political subjects and the spirit of liberty which had taken possession of the minds of the people ; and the forcible and direct manner in which the ministry always kept before their congregations the great and vital truths of the gospel.

CHAPTER VII.

CONTROVERSIES OF THE EARLY BAPTISTS OF VIRGINIA.

*Predestination and Arminianism. Classes of Baptists in England.
The immigration to Virginia of both classes. Their discussions
here. Division; action regarding it of Ketocton Association; of
Sandy Creek; of the General Association; of Kehuki; of the General
Committee. Reunion.*

THE Early Baptists of Virginia were not agreed in
their opinions on the doctrines of grace. Their differences on these subjects they inherited from their fathers
of the English churches. Those doctrines, subsequently
known in Ecclesiastical History as Calvinism and Arminianism, attracted, until the fourth century, very little attention. The controversies between Augustine
and Pelagius then brought them prominently forward.
Until the Lutheran Reformation, however, they were
confined for the most part to the schools, and produced
therefore no special public agitation. Before the Reformation, they did not disturb the harmony of Baptist
churches. After that period, they were regarded by
them as questions of much moment, and ultimately
divided them into two parties. In England, one of
these parties assumed the Arminian ground, and were
afterwards known as "General Baptists." The other
maintained the Calvinistic doctrine, and were denomi-
nated "Particular Baptists." Together they have always formed, as is well known, one of the most numer-

ous bodies of English Dissenters, and have counted among their number some of the ablest men, poets, orators and writers, that Britain ever produced. To say nothing of their laymen, such as Harrison, Ludlow, Lilbourne, Penn, and others, their list of ministers is singularly brilliant. The names of Tombes, Bampfield, Bunyan, Gosnold, Knollys, Denne, Cox, Jessey, Du Veil, Dell, Smyth, Helwisse, Barbour, Grantham, Russell, Gale, Emlyn, Whiston, Foster, Toulmin, Gifford, Steed, Vaux, Collins, Lamb, Price, Keats, Harris, Sutton, Adams, Mann, Harrison, the Stennetts, Piggott, Stinton, Delaune, Sharp, Gill, and a multitude of others would give fame to any denomination of Christians in any age or country.* Had these great men "agreed to disagree" on the doctrine of Predestination, and had their people mingled together freely in their devotional meetings as they did here, their differences would soon have been forgotten; and united they would have exerted an influence in favor of truth, of the extent and benefit of which they themselves probably never dreamed. Unhappily they kept up their collisions; were thrown asunder; and afterwards existed as two separate, and in some respects antagonistic, denominations.

The Baptist immigrants to Virginia came from both these classes. Here they all joined the same churches, mingled together indiscriminately, and while the churches were few and weak, lived together in unbroken harmony. When, however, Baptist principles began to extend, churches to multiply and flourish, and

* Benedict's Hist. Bapt., edit. 1848, pp. 320 et seq.

dangers and persecutions were to some extent withdrawn, their hereditary differences were again exhumed
and urged by their brethren in England, they again
separated from each other. Guided by "elective affinity," the churches were no longer one, but two. General Baptist churches and ministers, and Particular
Baptist churches and ministers, assumed their positions,
and without much discussion or agitation, not however
under these, but under new names. Their doctrines
were the same in Virginia as in Europe, but for some
reasons not now readily ascertained, they were here
known, not as General and Particular, but as Separate
and Regular Baptists, the former Arminian in senti-
timent, the latter Calvinistic.

Divided, however, as they were, these two classes of
Baptists still loved each other warmly and sincerely.
Essays were soon made to reunite them. These essays
were conducted mainly by the Associations, and with
great mutual kindness and respect, but unhappily without immediate success, although earnestly supported by
leading brethren on both sides. The first public movement in this direction was inaugurated by brethren in
1767, but received no very definite form. Three years
afterwards, in 1769, the Ketocton, a Regular, or Calvinistic Association in northern Virginia, addressed the
Sandy Creek, a Separate, or Arminian, Association in
southern Virginia, but mostly in North Carolina, on
this subject. Their letter was as follows:

"BELOVED IN OUR LORD JESUS CHRIST:

"The bearers of this letter [they were Rev.
Messrs. Garrett, Mager and Saunders] will acquaint

8*

you with the design of writing it. Their errand is peace, and their business is a reconciliation, if there is any difference subsisting. If we are all Christians, all Baptists, all New Lights,* why are we divided? Must the little appellatives, Regular and Separate, break the golden band of charity, and set the sons and daughters of God at variance? 'Behold how good and how pleasant it is for brethren to dwell together in unity!' But how bad and how bitter it is for them to live asunder and in discord! To indulge ourselves in prejudice is surely disorder, and to quarrel about nothing is irregularity with a witness. Oh, dear brethren, let us endeavor for the future to avoid this calamity."

The messengers were cordially received, the address was read, and the subject entertained and maturely considered. The proposed reunion received the concurrence of the body, but was deferred by an alleged necessity of settling with more deliberation some of its details. Of the original Sandy Creek Association, which then embraced in its district large portions of Virginia, North Carolina, and western South Carolina, this providentially was the last business session. It assembled the next year, but only to arrange for a separation into three kindred bodies. The churches in South Carolina agreed to meet for organization at Saluda; those in North Carolina, at Haw River, for a similar purpose; and those in Virginia, at Thompson's, Louisa County, where they were organized as the Rapid Ann Association in 1771, but were soon after merged as a body into the General Association of the Baptists of

---

* A recent name of reproach.

Virginia. Thus for a season the desired union failed; but some progress had evidently been made towards the object proposed.

We have seen, in a previous chapter, the organization of the General Association, with its peculiar character and object. In this body, both parties were members, and happily and harmoniously co-operated. At its second Annual Meeting, which was held in 1772, the subject of a re-union of the churches was brought up, and entertained, as entirely consonant with its designs. We have before seen that the Kehuki Association occupied, at this time, a part of South Carolina, the whole of lower North Carolina, and all that region of lower Virginia south of James River.* To this body the General Association addressed itself, and sent as messengers to confer with it on the subject, Samuel Harris, Elijah Craig, John Waller, and David Thompson, four of its ablest and most influential ministers. They attended the session, but with no success. Discussions on doctrinal subjects were provoked, and were conducted probably in a bad spirit. One of the impediments seems to have been that the General Association had published no Declaration of Faith. At its meeting in 1774, after the report of its messengers to the Kehuki, a "Question concerning a Confession of Faith" came up, and being maturely considered, that body decided that "A Confession of Faith is more proper for churches than for an Association."† However these

* Semple's Hist., &c., pp. 45–47. Burkett and Read's Hist. Kehuki Ass'n.

† Semple's Hist., &c., p. 55.

things might have been, the spirit of union now received a melancholy check, and for a short time division in that quarter, and not union, was industriously fomented.

Agitations and discussions regarding the Doctrines of Grace became general, and the session of the General Association itself for 1775 was rendered painfully memorable by their introduction into that body. Samuel Harris, Jeremiah Walker, and John Waller, defended the principles of the Separate Baptists, and William Murphy, John Williams, and Elijah Craig, sustained those of the Regular Baptists. Pamphlets had during the previous year been written and published by some of these gentlemen on both sides of the question at issue.* Great ability, candor, and Christian courtesy characterized these debates, which were continued a greater part of the session. The Association was called upon to express its opinion as to which of the contending parties was right, but the exact form of the question debated is not now of record, and cannot therefore be more definitely stated. At the close of the day on Monday a vote was had, and it was found that, by a very small majority, the sentiments of the Association were in favor of the Regular, or Predestinarian opinion, and adverse to that of the Separate, or Arminian doctrine. The decision was announced, and the Association adjourned amidst feelings of the most painful character. The minority were silent. The majority, after consulting together, determined to bring up the subject again the next day upon the

---

* These pamphlets I have not seen. No copies are accessible.

question, "Whether their opinions on these subjects should be made by the brethren on either side a bar to Christian fellowship and communion."

The General Association met on Tuesday. The two parties assembled apart, but in contiguous places. They opened communications with each other, all of which were conducted by messages, either verbal or written. The proceedings were exciting in the highest degree. The Regulars proposed to the Separates terms of union, which asked their assent to two propositions only; that "salvation is of the special electing grace of God;" and that "salvation is without merit on the part of the creature." To this message the Separates, after consultation, sent the following written response:—

"Dear Brethren: A steady union with you makes us willing to be more explicit in our answer to your terms of reconciliation proposed. We do not deny the former part of your proposition, respecting particular election of grace, still retaining our liberty with regard to construction. And as to the latter part, respecting merit in the creature, we are free to profess that there is none."

To this truly gratifying message, the Regulars sent the following Answer:—

"Dear Brethren: Inasmuch as your Christian fellowship seems nearly as dear to us as our lives, and seeing our difficulties concerning your principles with respect to merit in the creature, particular election, and final perseverance of saints are in a hopeful measure removing, we do willingly retain you in fellowship, not raising the least bar, but do heartily wish and pray that God in his kind providence in his own time may bring it to pass, when all Israel shall be of one mind, speaking the same things."

The effects of these communications were most happy. Both parties were deeply moved. By an instant and simultaneous movement they came joyfully together. Delight was in every heart. The Association restored to harmony, now resumed, finished its business, and adjourned.

The decision of the Association was universally approved by the brethren, and ratified by all the churches.* The reunion was, for the time, as happy as the conflict had been distressing. It was, however, not yet considered to be upon a basis as broad and stable as was desired. When, therefore, some years afterwards, the General Association, having as was believed accomplished its mission, was dissolved, and the General Committee, composed of chosen messengers from all the associations in the State, was instituted to take its place, much solicitude was felt on that subject. At the Annual meeting of that Committee for 1783, it came before the body, upon "A proposition to adopt a Confession of Faith." Why this measure was thought important, and why the General Committee—as its predecessor, the General Association, had done—did not decline it, we have now no data by which to determine. Serious apprehensions were felt and freely expressed, that the union between the Regular and

* Semple's History of the Virginia Baptists, pp. 60, 61.

Separate bodies was not—should the proposed measure be carried out—sufficiently strong to survive the shock it would receive. The Committee decided upon a middle course. It adopted " The Philadelphia Confession of Faith," but with such modifications and reservations as rendered it entirely unobjectionable. It was careful to affirm that, with its consent, none should be considered as obliged to embrace its teachings in all respects, and that " It should not usurp a tyrannical power over the conscience of any." The following are the recorded conditions : " We do not mean [in adopting this Confession of Faith] that every person is to be bound to the strict observance of everything therein contained; nor do we mean to make it in any respect superior, or equal to, the Scriptures in matters of faith and practice; all that we propose, is to express the opinion that it is the best human composition of the kind now extant; yet it shall be liable to alterations whenever the General Committee in behalf of the Association shall think fit." *

These proceedings evince several important facts. They show that all classes of Baptists in Virginia earnestly desired a solid and permanent union with each other ; that all their controversies were conducted in such a style and spirit as not seriously to jeopard this result; that the mutual personal bearing of the litigants was always singularly respectful and courteous ; that the high honor and Christian character of each other were invariably fully conceded ; that no one questioned the motives, purposes, or sincerity of another ;

* Semple's History, &c., pp. 59, 60.

that in their opinion Confessions of Faith were not proper for Associations; that when, after having been pressed to do so, the General Committee adopted the Philadelphia Confession of Faith, it was simply as an exposition, in general terms, of the leading principles which Baptists believe to be taught in the word of God, and not as a standard to govern them in their faith and practice; that all trials and other proceedings in the churches were directed by the Scriptures, and not by any human confession of faith; and that all these considerations met the universal favor of the churches and the people.

Notwithstanding all these proceedings, impediments to the permanent reunion of the two classes of Baptists in Virginia, of an embarrassing character, were continually springing up. The most formidable of these was found in the appeals supposed to have been addressed to the leading members of each class by their English brethren, to maintain here the separate organizations that had characterized their fathers in the Mother Country. Desirous to put these agitations forever to rest, the General Committee, at its session in 1786, adopted unanimously the following proceeding:

"It is recommended to the different Associations to appoint delegates to attend the next General Committee, for the purpose of forming a [more perfect] union" between the Separate and Regular Baptists of Virginia.*

The next annual meeting of the Committee was held at Dover, in Goochland County, and commenced Au-

* Semple's Hist. Va. Bap., p. 73.

gust 10th, 1787. In this meeting every Baptist Association in the State, without a single exception, was fully represented. The record of proceedings, as published by Semple, is as follows:*

"Agreeably to appointment the subject of the union of Regular [Particular] and Separate [General] Baptists was taken up," and referred to an able committee, to consider and report the conclusions at as early a period as practicable. In due time the committee reported, and after full consideration, "a happy and effectual reconciliation was accomplished." In the debates on the subject, the following considerations mainly occupied the meeting :—"The objections on the part of the Separates," says Dr. Semple, from whom this narrative is extracted, "related chiefly to matters of trivial importance, which had been for some time remedied." "On the other hand, the Regulars complained that the Separates were not sufficiently explicit in their principles, having never published nor sanctioned a Confession of Faith." "To these things it was answered by the Separates, that a large majority of them believed as much in their Confession of Faith as they did themselves; and that they did not approve the practice of churches binding themselves too strictly by Confessions of Faith, since there was danger that they might usurp finally too high a place; that if there were among them some who leaned too much towards the Arminian system, they were men of exemplary piety, and great usefulness in the Redeemer's kingdom; and that they conceived it better to bear with some diversity of opin-

* Hist., &c., pp. 74, 75.

ion in doctrine, than to break with men whose Christian deportment rendered them amiable in the estimation of all true lovers of genuine godliness; that some of them, indeed, had now become fathers in the gospel, who previous to the bias their minds had received, had borne the brunt and heat of persecution, whose labor and sufferings had been blessed and were still blessed to the great advancement of his cause; and that to exclude such as these from their communion would be like tearing the limbs from the body. These and such like arguments were agitated in public and in private, so that all minds were much conciliated before the final and successful attempts for union."

"The terms of the union," continues Dr. Semple, "were entered upon the minutes. They embraced the general recognition of the principles set forth in the Confession of Faith previously adopted, with the limitations and explanations before made by the General Association. After considerable debate as to the propriety of having a Confession of Faith at all, other than the Bible, the report of the committee was adopted, with the following addition. 'To prevent the Confession of Faith from usurping a tyrannical power over the conscience, we do not mean (by giving it our approval) that every person shall be bound to the strict observance of everything therein contained, but only that it holds forth the essential truths of the gospel, and (shows) that the doctrine of salvation by Christ, through free and unmerited grace alone, ought to be believed by every Christian, and maintained by every minister of the gospel. Upon these terms, we (such is the record) are *united;* and we desire that hereafter the names, Regular and Separate, shall be buried in oblivion ; and that henceforth we may be known by the name of The United Baptist Churches in Virginia.' "

These proceedings were adopted by all that immense and talented assembly, composed of both parties, unanimously. Every heart was thrilled with joy ; and as it went forth, it was hailed and ratified by the churches with inexpressible delight. All former party feelings were thenceforward banished ; the names, Regular and Separate, were heard no more ; all were practically as well as in name, "The United Baptist Churches in Virginia."

CHAPTER VIII.

EPISCOPACY AMONG THE EARLY BAPTISTS OF VIRGINIA.

Episcopacy adopted in Virginia. Its previous prevalence among English Baptists—Discussions on the subject. Institution of apostles. Its failure in practice. Its abandoment.

"THE early Baptists of Virginia," were strongly inclined to engraft upon their Church polity a peculiar form of Episcopacy. This bias arose in part from their former connection with the English General Baptists, and in part from the respect felt for that form of Ecclesiastical Government, by the great numbers of converts who had come to them from the Established Church, and who had been taught to believe that Episcopacy was of divine appointment.

Among the General Baptist churches of England, from which the churches in Virginia received large numbers of their members, Episcopacy prevailed, and at the time of the movement on that subject in the colony was received and acted upon as an institution of Christ.

The form of Episcopacy which prevailed in the General Baptist churches in England, is described by Dr. Wall, a distinguished writer of the English Episcopal Church. In his history of Infant Baptism Dr. Wall says:

"The General Baptists have some [ministers] whom

they call *Messengers*, which is the English word for *Apostles*. And there are of these, two sorts. Some are such of their Presbyters as being found of the best abilities, judgment, &c., are appointed (besides the care of their own congregations) to go sometimes about a certain district, diocese, or province. And when any of these come to preach in any other man's congregation, or to be present at any meeting of their churches, he is received and heard with greater respect than ordinary, and his authority more regarded than ordinary Presbyters. But for direct and proper jurisdiction over other Presbyters and people, he has none; nor any power of ruling but in his own congregation. The other sort is of such as are nothing else but Messengers, in the ordinary sense of the English word, viz., men appointed as messengers to carry the sense and opinions of some congregations to other congregations at a distance." *

Doubtless, however, Baptist writers are on such subjects more reliable than others. To them we turn for our authorities. Richard Taylor, on this subject, observes :—

" Ever attentive to the teachings of the word of God, it was not long before they (the General Baptists of England) supposed that they discovered in the primitive churches an officer superior to an elder. They remarked that Barnabas, Luke, Timothy, Titus, and several others were fellow-laborers with the Apostles in the preaching of the gospel and the planting and regulating of churches; and that in various passages

* Hist. Inf. Bap. part 2, chap. 8, Lects. 6 and 20.

they were called *Apostles*, or in English *Messengers*, of the churches. They thought it probable that the angels, or messengers, of the seven churches in Asia, to whom the author of the Revelation addressed his epistles, were also of the same order. They, therefore, introduced an officer into their system whom they styled a *Messenger*. He was generally chosen by an Association of the representatives of the churches in a certain district, and ordained by those of his own order with great solemnity, the various churches keeping seasons of prayer and fasting. Sometimes a particular church chose a Messenger; but in that case his business appears to have been confined to preaching the gospel where it was not known; and regulating such churches as he might be instrumental in planting. It is indeed probable that at the first this was the chief object of their appointment ; an object which demanded peculiar attention when the nation was just emerging from the darkness of Popery and Prelacy, and the rays of divine truth had hardly pierced the gloom. Fixed pastors could not conveniently itinerate in distant parts; and it would have been thought irregular for unauthorized persons to have undertaken it; but the Messengers stood ready for this necessary work, and their office called them to it."

Speaking of these Messengers, or if you please, Apostles, or Bishops, Mr. Jeffrey observes :—"They were appointed for the gathering of churches, and the establishment of them." "But when churches increased [in numbers] and errors and irregularities sprung up among the young converts and inexperienced ministers, it was judged expedient to extend the Messenger's work by assigning him the superintendence, and in a sense the government, of the churches which united in calling them to the office."

In the Confession of Faith of the General Baptists of 1678, the duties of these officers are explicitly described as follows:—"The bishops had the government of those churches that had suffrage in their election; and no others ordinarily; as also to preach the word to the world."

Mr. Grantham says of these bishops:—"Their ministry is, 1, To plant churches where there are none; 2, To set in order such churches as want officers to order their affairs; 3, To assist faithful pastors or churches against usurpers and such as trouble the peace of particular churches by false doctrine."

Mr. Hook is explicit as to the prerogatives of these Baptist bishops. He says they were, "To plant churches; ordain officers; set in order things that are wanting in all the churches; to defend the gospel against gainsayers; and to travel up and down the world for this purpose." *

Such was English Baptist Episcopacy, as to its origin, character, purposes, and prerogatives. From these General Baptist churches, many immigrated, ministers and laymen, and united with the churches in Virginia. They, of course, brought with them their traditional feelings and preferences, and were desirous to see the churches in their new homes conform to those

---

* See Benedict's History of the Baptists, pp. 332, 333, et seq. edition in one vol.

they loved so much in Britain. But Episcopacy here had also another source, by the influence of which that of the English Baptists, when adopted in Virginia, had engrafted upon it decidedly more of the diocesan character.

Very great numbers of the Early Baptists of Virginia had been reared and educated in the Episcopal Church. The impressions of childhood are in after years effaced with great difficulty. Experimentally and practically, they had "learned the way of the Lord more perfectly." Ecclesiastical Polity they had never investigated. They did not, therefore, see why Episcopacy should not obtain among Baptists. They had been accustomed to a hierarchy, and to admit as Scriptural and conclusive the arguments by which it was sustained. Now that the love of Christ had been shed abroad in their hearts, they were greatly anxious to do and sustain whatever appeared to them to be his will. Was Episcopacy really Scriptural and divinely appointed? Then they desired to adopt and practice it. Their motives and purposes were undoubtedly of the purest character.

During several years, this was a subject of much conversation among both the ministers and the people, and sometimes found a place in their public discourses. In 1774, the General Association in annual session received and sustained the following "Query," which brought the whole matter directly before that body :—

"Ought all the ministerial gifts recorded in Ephesians iv. 11, 12, 13, to be in use at the present time?"

"He gave some apostles, and some prophets, and some evangelists, and some pastors and teachers; for the perfecting of the saints; for the work of the ministry; for the edifying of the body of Christ: till we all come in the unity of the faith, and of the knowledge of the Son of God, unto a perfect man, to the measure of the stature of the fulness of Christ."

Long and anxious deliberations, expositions, and discussions ensued, and the following answer was at length adopted: "A great majority suppose, that all the ministerial gifts recorded in the said Scriptures are, and ought to be, still in use in the churches. But we pay due regard to the distinction between ordinary and extraordinary gifts."*

By this action of the General Association, the advocates of Episcopacy had obtained a recognition of the principle, although in general and rather evasive terms. Their confidence that now they could induce the brethren to carry it into practice was complete. To that body they looked as possessing the requisite authority to this end. At its Annual Meeting in 1775, the subject was again brought up by a query, as follows: "If the ministerial gifts of apostolic times be still in use, ought they not to be recognized and instituted by the churches in Virginia?"

Two days were occupied in the debate on this query, which took a very wide range, embracing the whole subject of Episcopacy in the various phases which it has assumed among Catholics, Episcopalians, and Baptists. A motion was then made that the whole subject

---

* Semple's Hist. Va. Baptists, p. 50.

be laid upon the table "until the next Association," to give time for its more full consideration.* This motion was carried by a majority, and accordingly the decision was postponed for a year. This whole period was occupied by the ministers in earnest discussions, and especially upon the question, whether it was not their duty to revive the office of "Apostle," otherwise known as Messenger, or Bishop, and ordain suitable men to the discharge of its duties. Jeremiah Walker, who was its ablest advocate, wrote and published a pamphlet in its support, entitled "Free Thoughts," which had a very wide circulation. In this work he presented with much skill and eloquence the usual arguments employed by Episcopalians in defence of Prelacy, and which may be found in any of the works by writers of that school on Ecclesiastical Polity. The ablest opponent of the measure was Reuben Ford. He also wrote and published a pamphlet, not inferior to the other, designed to refute the arguments of Mr. Walker, and which had a circulation equally wide.† The public mind became during the year intensely excited on the subject.

The General Association of 1776 met in Annual Session. As was expected, the messengers present were very numerous. After the usual preliminary services, the all-absorbing proposition was called up, and its discussion again commenced. In the process of the debate, by order of the Association, the pamphlets on

---

* Semple's Hist. Va. Baptists, p. 57.

† I have been unable to find these pamphlets. Are they irrecoverably lost? Are they not still among Dr. Semple's papers?

both sides, above referred to, were read in the presence of the whole body. A vote was finally decided upon. The question as stated by the Moderator was: "Are the said offices now in use in Christ's Church?" The votes were taken, and it was found that all but three were in the affirmative. These three immediately arose, and changed their votes. The decision of the body was, therefore, recorded as "unanimously in the affirmative."

Another proposition was now presented, as follows: "The General Association will proceed immediately to establish the said offices by the appointment and ordination of proper persons to fill them."

This proposition elicited no debate, and was decided in the affirmative by a unanimous vote. It will be noticed, however, that the subsequent action of the association was not in consonance with either of the propositions it had adopted! They both include the offices, not of Apostles only, but also of Prophets, Evangelists, and of Teachers. They had just decided to "establish said *offices*, by the appointment of proper persons to fill *them!*" Pastors they had of course, but they appointed no persons to fill the offices of Prophets, nor of Evangelists, nor of Teachers! These, although they had voted to establish them, they did not establish! They seem to have never been impressed with the idea, that, according to the terms of all the queries, and all the propositions, these offices were included; or to have now forgotten them entirely; and to have thought only of the apostleship.

The Association on motion, decided to appoint and

ordain an Apostle ; and at present, but one only; and
that the election should be conducted by private ballot.
The votes were cast, and on being counted it was
found that Samuel Harris was unanimously elected an
apostle.

The next day was, by order, set apart for the ordination of Mr. Harris, and the services were conducted
with great solemnity. It was decided that the whole
day should be observed by the entire Association as a
solemn fast, in which the congregation was requested
to unite. The Association assembled at an early hour,
and proceeded with the ordination services. Various
hymns were sung, appropriate Scriptures read, and
prayer was offered successively by John Waller, Elijah
Craig, and John Williams. The Apostle elect was
placed in a central position ; the Presbytery on the occasion embraced all the preachers present, and in his
formal inauguration, by the Moderator, while the
words of investment and benediction were being pronounced, the hands of every ordained minister in the
body were laid upon him. The members then returned to their seats; Mr. Harris stood in his place,
and John Waller addressed to him a solemn charge—
setting forth the nature of his duties, the fearful re-
sponsibilities he had assumed, and the necessity of hu-
mility, watchfulness, prayer, and scrupulous fidelity—
characterized by all the great ability and fervor for
which that gentleman was distinguished. The right
hand of fellowship, while an appropriate hymn was
being sung, was then extended to Mr. Harris, successively by every member of the Association, and the

formalities of the ordination, which had occupied nearly the whole day, closed. The diocese of this new Apostle was then designated. It embraced the whole of that part of Virginia which lies south of the James River. The Association, with the usual devotional forms, then adjourned for the day.

Thus was inaugurated and sent forth, commended to the grace of God by all his brethren, the first Baptist Bishop of Virginia. Unhappily he was not the last. The people warmly approved this movement, and were impatient for the appointment of other Bishops to occupy the remaining portion of the State. The Association was, therefore, by general request, called together, in the autumn of the same year, to consider, and if thought prudent, to act upon the subject. It assembled accordingly, and with the forms observed in the case of Mr. Harris, elected and ordained two other Apostles, John Waller, and Elijah Craig. Their diocese was fixed together, and embraced all that part of the State north of the James River.

At this meeting the duties assigned to the Apostles, and in case of their committing sins, the discipline to be observed in regard to them, were fixed and recorded by the Association. The *duties* assigned them were as follows:—"To pervade the churches; to do or at least to see to the work of ordination; to set in order the things that are wanting; and to make report to the next Association." The *discipline* appointed was recorded thus:—"If our Messenger, or Apostle, shall transgress in any manner, he shall be liable to dealing in any church where the transgression is com-

10

mitted, and the said church is instructed to call helps from two or three neighboring churches; and if by them convicted of the offence, a General Conference of the churches shall be called to excommunicate or to restore him."*

The revolution in Church Polity among the early Baptists of Virginia is now complete. It was achieved, not without much excitement and discussion, but without any division. The circumstances that surrounded them did not admit of division; their political influence, not to say their safety, would have been endangered by it; they could not successfully resist the revolution; they therefore, accepted it unanimously. The General Association had assumed powers not exceeded by any previous body of clergy in any age, Catholic or Protestant. Not only had it created and sent forth three diocesan Bishops, under the name of "Apostles, or Messengers," but it had taken them, unlike the English Baptists, from the jurisdiction of the individual churches of which they were members, to whose discipline they were no longer subject; ordination of ministers was removed from the churches and given to the Bishops; it instructed the churches how to proceed in case they should commit offences demanding their impeachment; and if in this Lower court an indictment was sustained, it provided for the organization of a High court, to be called "A General Conference of the Churches," which should have power "to excommunicate or restore them." All this was monstrous, but we will not now pursue the subject. We proceed

* Semple's History of the Virginia Baptists, pp. 58, 59.

to consider the practical workings of this new system.

The Bishops entered without delay upon the discharge of their duties. Meantime, by what means is
not known now, a reaction had taken place in public
sentiment on that subject. Their services were not
cordially accepted by the churches. Animadversions,
although apparently too late, were renewed, and pro-
secuted with increased earnestness and solicitude. The
whole scheme was now thoroughly canvassed by the
people, not under the influence of fervid addresses
from the pulpit, but calmly and in the light of the
gospel. The auspices were very different. The most
able and eloquent advocates of Episcopacy, whose great
personal influence and extraordinary powers of persuasion especially carried the measure, had already retired from the field. They were suspected, whether
justly or unjustly, of having been themselves desirous
of reaching the apostleship. None of them were
elected to this high office. No longer mingling in the
discussion, the public mind was left to the full influence of such counter arguments as were presented.
The gentlemen themselves who had been ordained
Bishops, were characterized by great modesty, sincerity, and piety. They had much more of conscien-
tiousness than ambition ; and they were not very con-
fident that their office, and much less that the changes
in Church Government, consequent upon its institution,
were justified by the word of God. They were not,
therefore, solicitous to retain their positions. Now for
the first time since its agitation, the circumstances sur-

rounding it, and the state of the public mind were favorable to a full and impartial investigation of the subject. It was so investigated, and the results were most salutary. These results may be briefly stated.

It was ascertained that Episcopacy is derived from the Old Temple service under the Mosaic dispensation, as Presbytery is from the Synagogue system which prevailed in the later ages of the Hebrew Commonwealth; and that both are therefore forms of Judaism, which Christian churches cannot adopt without a departure from the gospel, and consequent irreparable injury; that by the law of Christ all Christians individually are priests; that Christ himself is the perpetual and only High-priest; and that priesthood in any sense not common to Christians generally, does not as such enter at all into the Christian ministry; that the Apostles, as soon as they had planted and confirmed the churches, induced them each to appoint their own pastors and teachers, who were their bishops in the true, legitimate gospel sense, each being bishop of a single church, and no more, and invested with apostolical authority in all respects in which that authority ever was transmitted to successors; that instances occurred in apostolic times in which individual churches (congregations) had two or more bishops, being very numerous, but in no case that a single bishop presided over two or more churches; that each church (single congregation) was, under Christ, sovereign and independent; that it was not subject to any power of an earthly character outside of itself, civil or ecclesiastical; and that this sovereignty and independence, being conferred upon them for special purposes, were inalienable; that, therefore, the churches, even if they had desired it, could not create, as a governing body, the General Association nor any other like organization; that all the proceedings of that body in this affair were unscriptural, a dangerous usurpation, and such as ought to be resisted, overthrown, and abolished; that the Apostles of our Lord Jesus Christ were appointed as such, not only to preach, to teach, and administer ordinances—duties which other ministers, not Apostles, performed in common with them, but especially as witnesses to bear testimony to the doctrines he taught, the miracles he performed, his death, his burial, his resurrection, his ascension, and the descent of the Holy Spirit; that, therefore, it was an essential qualification of an Apostle that he should have personally seen our Lord Jesus Christ, and been instructed by him; that the Apostles, under the guidance of inspiration, recorded their testimony in the several books that make up the New Testament, and that so far as their authority was peculiar, it was transmitted and perpetuated, not by men, but by that inspired record; that from the very nature of the office as there could, after that record was completed, be no further need for Apostles, so it was impossible that the twelve could have had any official successors; that the persons designated by the Apostles themselves to fill their places as far as they could be filled, were the Christian pastors, teachers, and evangelists; that these, as the ministers of the word and ordinances, were to be perpetuated by the churches themselves, and not by bodies apart from them, and acting as either above

10*

them, or as having any authority to direct or control their actions; and that thus the gospel was to be perpetuated and extended until the whole world should be converted to God. These great truths and principles became gradually but surely fixed in the minds of the people, and produced a powerful and lasting impression. The newly appointed Apostles themselves partook largely of the feeling of the masses on this subject. The tide had turned, and now ran rapidly in the other direction.

Such was the state of feeling under which the General Association assembled the next year. The Apostles reported in desponding terms. The churches had not solicited, and they felt disinclined to press their services upon them; they had in their quality as Bishops done nothing. Their reports elicited no remarks. No action of the Association was had regarding them. All parties seem to have been willing to drop the subject; nothing further was said; they were evidently desirous to forget all that they had done. The Apostles ceased to act as such altogether. In a very short time the whole thing fell into desuetude. Without any rescinding action, or other adverse movement officially taken, the Episcopacy was tacitly abandoned. Once only afterwards do we hear of the subject. At a subsequent annual session of the General Association, we find upon its Journal the following record:—

"*Resolved*, That the office of Apostles, like that of Prophets, was the effect of miraculous inspiration, and does not belong to our times." *

* Semple's Hist. Va. Baptists, p. 59.

This resolution was accompanied by some explanation, but elicited almost no discussion, and was adopted unanimously. All the churches and people were gratified. The Bishops retired from their unscriptural elevation, and gladly resumed their places beside their brother Presbyters. Such were the origin, progress, and end of Episcopacy among the Early Baptists of Virginia.

CHAPTER IX.

CAUSES OF THE REUNION AMONG THE EARLY BAPTISTS OF VIRGINIA.

Discordances to be overcome. Union in a few vital principles. Ardent Christian love. Their indiscriminate persecutions. The political ends they mutually sought.

NEVER has any denomination reached a more perfect union within itself than was at last attained by the Early Baptists of Virginia. This happy result was the more remarkable when we consider the discordance of the materials of which their churches were originally composed. Their ministers, who preached before they united with them, were gathered from five denominations, the General Baptists and the Particular Baptists of England, the Congregationalists and Presbyterians of New England, and Episcopalians of the Established Church of Virginia; their members were mainly from three—the first two, and the last named. To shake off all the prejudices of earlier years, to abandon former preferences, and readily to fall in with new doctrines, forms, and associations, is proverbially difficult. It is well known that the Baptist churches of the American States, although in some respects they have been greatly benefited, in other respects have been seriously injured, by the great influx of ministers from all the surrounding churches, who within the present century, have pressed into their constantly thickening ranks. Especially have they suffered in the purity of doctrine, and the simplicity of their gospel Church Government. Precisely so was it in Virginia. We have seen in former chapters, the divisions and agitations and conflicts through which they passed on both these subjects. Churches ought not to be desirous of receiving persons into their membership more rapidly than they can be instructed, disciplined, and formed into a homogeneous mass. Especially ought they to be slow to admit ministers,

" Who cannot teach, and will not learn."

Reference has before been made to the independence of mind and fervor of feeling which characterized the people of Virginia. They had their own convictions on all subjects, and they maintained them firmly at whatever hazard ; nor were they afraid to carry them out practically. When fairly convinced that they were in error, but never otherwise, they would readily abandon every false way, and ingenuously confess their aberrations. They had as much pride in abandoning an error, as in maintaining the truth.

When all these facts are considered—their diversity of origin, their differences in doctrine, their discrepancies on Church Polity, their actual separations—it is wonderful that they were not entirely alienated ; and their divisions were not permanently maintained. Some powerful causes must have been in action to prevent such results. To some of these causes we will now refer.

The first was a profound conviction of the importance of a few grand principles in which they all stood together.

These were, the necessity of repentance towards God and faith in our Lord Jesus Christ, in order to the remission of sins; regeneration the work of the Holy Spirit in the soul of the believer; church membership confined to professed believers in our Lord Jesus Christ; baptism or the Lord's Supper never the medium of regeneration or the conferring of the Holy Ghost, but in every case declarative only of the faith of the recipient; and the duty of keeping the church pure by a strict exercise of discipline in the church itself over its own members. Whatever might be their differences on other subjects, on these vital points they were, always had been, and always continued to be a perfect unity. Their warm agreement here, and their high appreciation of the importance to true religion of the principles involved, doubtless had much to do in holding them together in despite of all their conflicts, and securing at last a perfect and permanent reunion.

A second cause may be found in the ardent Christian feeling which, as a whole, characterized the Early Baptists of Virginia.

Their congregations were almost perpetually in a state of revival. Brotherly love burned in their hearts. They were often side by side at the Lord's table in each other's churches. No worldly ambition or jealousies existed among them. Literally, as to personal religion, "each esteemed other better than himself." None of them of either party, Predestinarians or Arminians, Independents or Prelatists, sought for themselves earthly distinctions, emolument, or place, but only the glory of God, the triumph of truth, and the salvation of men. It was not, therefore, difficult for them to harmonize on any other subject connected with the religion of Christ.

A third cause of their perfect and permanent reunion was undoubtedly the indiscriminate persecutions waged against them all alike by the State Church.

All parties suffered together; all suffered alike; and all suffered as Baptists. Whether General Baptists or Particular Baptists, or as the same parties were afterwards called, Separate Baptists or Regular Baptists; or whether they were the advocates or the opponents of the mooted Episcopacy; it made no difference with their determined pursuers. The leaders, lay and ministerial, of all parties found themselves together in the hands of the State officers; before the Courts of law; and in the prisons of the several counties, charged with the crime of holding conventicles, preaching to the people, and other similar heinous offences against the peace and dignity of the Commonwealth. These companionships necessarily produced powerful results, both upon the men themselves, who thereby became personally strongly endeared to each other, and upon their friends everywhere, whose sympathies all ran in the same channel. To these facts references were constantly made in all their negotiations with each other looking to reunion. This was doubtless the feeling which prompted that affecting remark, before noticed, contained in one of their official communications, in which one party, in answer to an earnest overture for union, said to the other party sending it:

"Your Christian fellowship seems nearly as dear to us as our lives."

How could two such parties remain asunder? Nothing is more natural or more inevitable than that such men, under such circumstances, whatever their original differences, should come together, and that their union should be as complete and as harmonious as any of which imperfect human beings are capable.

The last cause which need now be mentioned, was the necessity of concentrating all their influence and efforts to gain those political ends, for the attainment of which, especially, the General Association was organized.

What these ends were, we shall have occasion to explain more fully when we come to examine the influence of the Baptists of Virginia in the formation of the government of the State, in destroying the connection between the Government and the Established Church, and in the final repeal of all laws infringing religious freedom and denominational equality. In the General Association all classes of Baptists mingled, and always did mingle together on equal and common ground. If divided and in conflict with each other, with their energies enfeebled and their powers thus prostituted and debased, what could they have hoped to accomplish? Nobly did they spurn such petty warfare, and generously did they unite their forces to achieve the most happy results. No one sacrificed a particle of principle. Happily no such sacrifice was either necessary or demanded. The diversities among them were found to be no greater than are usually found among the members of the same church, and to deal with which is never thought to be necessary or beneficial. They all became one harmonious and gallant army, which now marched forward in its strength, conquering and to conquer.

These, with the blessing of Almighty God, were some of the chief causes which led to the reunion of the Early Baptists of Virginia. Regular and Separate Baptists, as such, were known no more. Apostleship, as an office in the church in our time, except as a vagary into which for a short period the fathers had at one time unhappily fallen, ceased to be remembered. All were United Baptists, not in name only, but also "in deed and in truth."

CHAPTER X.

EVILS THAT PREVAILED AMONG THE EARLY BAP-TISTS OF VIRGINIA.

The failure of their educational plans. Their mistakes regarding the use of money as a means of extending religion. Their conduct as to wealth and social position. Their neglect in regard to books. Their carelessness in reference to centres of influence. Their errors regarding the unaided force of truth. Injudicious ordinations of ministers.

SEEDS of evil were early sown among the Baptists of Virginia which subsequently sprung up, and have produced much bitter fruit. Nearly all the perplexities and injuries with which during the present century they have had to contend, had then their incipient beginning. To some of these, fidelity requires that we shall briefly refer.

1. The Early Baptists of Virginia failed, unhappily, to take their proper part in the education of the people of the State.

This failure resulted disastrously in various ways, some of which we will briefly designate. It is proper, however, to say that it did not arise from any want of interest on the general subject. They fully appreciated education for themselves and others. They also moved in the matter at a very early day, as early at least as the Presbyterians, who have since regarded themselves as the special patrons of learning. We will present a sketch of their proceedings on that subject.

The interests of education claimed for the first time

publicly the attention of the denomination in 1788. The General Committee held its annual session at Du Puy's, in August of that year. A letter to that body from Dr. Manning, President of Providence College, now Brown University, in Rhode Island, was laid before it. That letter has never been published, and is therefore, if it exists at all, not accessible to the present writer. Its contents may be understood by the action of the Committee to which it led. After the reading and consideration of the letter, the following resolution was unanimously adopted:

"*Resolved,* That a committee of [ten members] five persons on each side of James River be appointed to forward the business respecting a seminary of learning."

This committee was composed of the ablest and most influential Baptists in the Commonwealth. Those on the south side of the river were Samuel Harris, John Williams, Eleazer Clay, Simeon Walton, and David Barrow; and those of the north side of the river were Robert Carter, John Waller, William Fristoe, John Leland, and Reuben Ford.

The annual meeting of the Committee for the next year was held in the city of Richmond. The committee on "A Seminary of Learning" reported. That report has not been preserved, and therefore its contents cannot be stated. All that is of record is that the committee, with several changes in its membership, was reappointed, with instructions to exert itself with reference to the important interests committed to its care, and to report the next year. Three years past, and although the subject was annually called up, and discussed, no progress was made by the committee.

The meeting of the General Committee for 1793 was held at Muddy Creek, in Powhattan County. Here the subject was again discussed, and the enterprise warmly advocated by several members. The old committee was discharged, and on motion, Rev. John Williams and Thomas Reid, Esq., of Charlotte, were appointed to prepare, and submit during the session, a plan for the proposed school. These gentlemen reported the next day, and proposed as follows:—

"That the General Committee now appoint fourteen trustees, all of whom shall be Baptists; that these fourteen at their first meeting appoint seven others, who shall be of other denominations; and that the whole twenty-one trustees then form a plan for the desired Seminary, and make arrangements for its execution."

This report was adopted; the fourteen trustees proposed were appointed; some weeks afterwards they met, and appointed the additional seven; they devised a plan to carry the school into operation; some funds were necessary for buildings and other purposes; they set about collecting them; they failed to obtain a sufficient amount; they so reported to the General Committee at its next annual meeting; and here for the time the whole matter terminated.

The enterprise was not again called up for fifteen years, and then in a modified form. At the annual meeting of the General Meeting of Correspondence, held at Tarwallet, commencing October 20th, 1809, it was proposed to "establish some Seminary or Public

School, to assist young preachers to acquire literary knowledge." The project was favorably entertained, and "two members were appointed to acquire information and digest a plan for such a seminary." So far as is now known, "no report was ever made, and no further action was had." * The Virginia Baptists are indeed now not behind the very foremost denomination in the number and efficiency of their colleges and other schools, but to refer more fully to them would carry us too far beyond the chronological limits prescribed to these brief chapters. These facts are not reputable to the Early Baptists of Virginia, but they are due to the truth of history, and are here adduced to show that they were not indifferent to the value and importance of education to the people generally, and to ministers especially.

1. This failure lost to them, and placed in the hands of their opponents, one among the most effectual of all the means that are used for the advancement of denominational interests.

So cordially did the Baptists abhor all proselyting, that they refused to employ education as an auxiliary to denominational advancement. They despised sectarianism of every character, and looked with loathing upon any man who would use his influence as a teacher to give a denominational bias to the minds of his pupils. In all these respects their sentiments were exalted and noble, but they carried them too far. They retired, to a great extent, from the field of education, and left it in the hands of others, who had no

---

* Semple's History of the Virginia Baptists, pp. 77, 89.

such scruples as governed them, but who employed all these means, and to the utmost extent, for their own denominational advantage. With the reputation of being intensely sectarian, the Baptists were then, and are now, the most unsectarian class of Christians in the country. Very few of them sought places as teachers in any of the Academies, Colleges, or Universities of the State. The education of the people was, therefore, left in the hands of the sects around them, and especially of the Presbyterians, the smallest and weakest of them all. These sects carried with them, therefore, a large portion of the educated classes, and among them not a few of the children of Baptists themselves.

By this failure, the Baptists incurred the reproach of being the enemies of education.

This slander was, for sectarian purposes, industriously propagated, and especially among the young people in their schools. The Baptists took no pains to remove it. The people at last believed it. It became stereotyped. The pulpit and the press boldly declared it. The practical effect was crushing. The educated classes were turned away from them, and it was pitiful to see the descendants of those very men who had been imprisoned, fined, and whipped by Pedobaptists for their principles, now in league with their very persecutors, and leading members of the identical churches which so bitterly pursued and punished their fathers! The injurious results of this one source of evil, who can fully estimate?

2. The early Baptists of Virginia failed to perceive the true relation between religion and the use of money as a means for its advancement.

We can readily trace the sources of this error, but the consequences were not on that account the less disastrous. The Episcopal clergy, supported by the State, were generally mere hirelings. The salaries they received were their only motive for preaching. When that was withheld they preached no more. The Baptists, with other citizens of the State, were taxed to make up these salaries, and compelled to pay the assessment. The Presbyterian clergy, though sustained by their own congregations, were the advocates of taxation by the State for the support of religion, and they made long and strenuous efforts to secure for their own churches a share in the support thus created. The Baptists alone, as we shall hereafter see, were the advocates of "The voluntary principle," and for a series of years they maintained it in opposition to all other denominations. In their conflicts against the union of Church and State, and the measures adopted by the Government for the support of religion ; and in their infinite disgust, created by the course of all classes of Pedobaptist ministers and churches in regard to it, so intensely excited did they become, that they could see but one side of the subject, and were, therefore, betrayed into a most injurious extreme. Partly on these accounts, and partly to be above even the suspicion of mercenary motives, many of their ministers refused all pecuniary compensation whatever for their services, and not one would consent to any fixed salary from the church of which he was pastor. Several consequences resulted of an injurious character, to which we will barely allude.

One of these consequences was an almost entire withdrawal of money from the list of instrumentalities, to be used for the advancement of the cause of Christ. The people were left without any adequate instruction on this subject. The mention of money always brought up to their minds the Harpies of the State Church, their harassments in reference to taxation, and the Judases of all classes, who sell their Lord for paltry silver. They were not, indeed, instructed to hoard money, or to refuse to give liberally to any cause which they believed worthy; but generally they were rather encouraged to withhold it altogether from all religious projects. As a consequence, any enterprise among Baptists which required the use of money, beyond the building of a meeting-house, or the support of the poor of the church, was for many years almost impossible. To this cause undoubtedly is due the failure in both instances, of the educational designs of 1788 and 1809, to which we have before referred.

Another of these evil consequences, was the failure of the churches adequately to support their pastors. This failure became a prolific source of disasters. Obliged to provide for his family as best he could, by his own personal labors, the pastor had no time either to read extensively or to prepare carefully for the pulpit; or beyond a sermon on Lord's Day, to perform any pastoral work whatever; only the wealthy could devote themselves to the ministry, without bringing suffering and distress upon the loved ones at home; young men qualified, by the possession of piety and talents, for the work of the ministry, and doubtless called to it by God, resisted, and in most cases successfully, their sense of duty, and never preached. The prospect of a life of laborious toil, unrequited anxiety, and of certain poverty with all its concomitants, which the Baptist ministry of that day presented to them, was sufficiently repulsive. No one entered it who could do otherwise, and satisfy his conscience; and even the sermons preached were too often, since the ministers had no time to prepare them, necessarily superficial and feeble. Under such influences as these, the churches of no denomination could long continue to be successful.

Yet another injury arising from a failure of the Baptist Fathers to perceive the true relations between religion and the use of money as a means of its advancement, was the countenance thus given to some most odious imputations, constantly heaped upon them by their adversaries. It was everywhere charged, that as a whole, and individually, Baptists were close, penurious, covetous, narrow-hearted men. That these charges would justly apply to no Baptists of that day, it is not necessary to affirm, but that it was characteristic of them generally as a class, was most false and unjust. In common with the citizens of Virginia generally, they were known to be profuse in their hospitality; when money was wanted for any patriotic, moral, or social purposes, their contributions were as liberal and as cheerfully made as those of any of their neighbors. In no respect did they in ordinary matters differ from their fellow-citizens of the

other denominations.   Why then did they not sustain
their pastors, and carry on vigorously among themselves other religious enterprises ?   Was it their fault
that they failed in these respects?   Certainly not.
These very pastors had instilled into their minds
strong prejudices against the use of money for any
such purposes.   They were themselves the sufferers,
and the churches and the cause suffered irretrievably.

3. The manner in which the rich and aristocratic
among the Early Baptists of Virginia habitually expressed themselves in society regarding their churches
and ministers, proved to be an evil of very great magnitude.

The ministry and churches of that day were not, to
any great extent, nor are those of the present day, composed of the elite, par excellence, who revel in luxury,
and pride themselves, not upon their own personal
talents and powers, but upon the exalted position and
great deeds of a long since buried ancestry.   The Baptists were the masses of the people.   "Not many rich,
not many noble," were among them.   They counted
in their membership, as all true churches ever will,
many of the "poor, who were rich in faith and heirs of
the kingdom," who generally proved the truest, most
useful, and best friends of the cause.   Of the rich, the
proud, and the high-born, the churches contained but
too many for their own happiness and prosperity.
The countenance which these classes gave to the aspersions of their enemies, imparted to them all the power
of mischief they ever had.   Men and women of this
class, whose hearts God by his Holy Spirit had

changed, were compelled by stress of. conscience, to unite with the churches. They did so, and all their lifetime afterwards, were unhappily on every occasion boasting of the sacrifices they had thereby made—sacrifices of society, friendships, and the refinements of social life! To talk of "the poor Baptists" whom they had joined for the sake of truth; to tell anecdotes of the awkwardness and illiteracy of some of their ministers, whom they had seen or of whom they had heard; to detail the opposition of their families, or of their friends, to their "throwing themselves away" by · joining the Baptists, became with them a passion. Strange as it may seem, this spirit assumed epidemical form, and pervaded all classes; it found expression even from the pulpit; it was reiterated from the very obscurest of the members, who it seems were anxious to be in fashion with their more cultivated brethren! Upon their own minds the effect was most melancholy, since they could not cherish a warm regard for persons whose character and position they were ever disparaging. Upon the minds of their children the results were much worse. Generally they had no respect for Baptist ministers, and seldom heard them preach; Baptist people they regarded as unfit society for them; and when they professed religion, very often joined consequently other denominations, who were perhaps really less cultivated, intelligent, and wealthy than the Baptists! Such were the outrageous calumnies which were originated among themselves; which were perpetuated in certain quarters; and which other denominations delighted to repeat, and extend; and such were the terrible results to which they led. It would be unjust, however, to the memory of the Fathers, should we fail to add, that this temper was not indulged by all the rich, the exalted, and the cultivated of that day, nor indeed by those who partook most of these characteristics. Not a few there were in the churches, in whose veins coursed the blood of the proudest Cavaliers in the Commonwealth, who loved the Saviour, his cause, and his people too much to allow themselves to speak and act thus foolishly. It is proper here to say that the Baptists as a whole, were in all respects, equal at least, to the same number of men and women, taken promiscuously from society in this or any other country.

4. Their carelessness in defending the honor of their churches and people was another evil which prevailed among the Early Baptists of Virginia.

The Lord gave them, as we have seen, with some internal agitations and conflicts, extraordinary prosperity. On this account, and on some others, they were greatly envied and hated by the sects around them, by whom they were perpetually attacked and defamed. Reproaches of the gravest character were consequently cast upon them. To some of these we have referred. But these were not all. It was charged, that as a class, the Baptists were disreputably ignorant; that they refused to be enlightened; that their ministers generally were raving fanatics; that they were penurious and narrow-minded; that they were of questionable moral habits; that they paid no regard to the moral training of their children; and many other imputations of a similar character! These falsehoods poured in an unending stream from the pulpit and from the press. That Baptists should feel for them the profoundest contempt was very natural. Hence only an occasional reference was made to them in any of their public meetings. An instance occurred at the Annual Session of the General Meeting of Correspondence in 1808. Dr. Semple says:—*

"It appeared from some late publications, that the Baptists in Virginia had been misrepresented as to their sentiments respecting human learning. It was determined at this meeting, to rebut this calumny by publishing a few remarks on that subject, in the form of a circular letter, which was accordingly done."

But who read that fugitive "Circular Letter?" Probably a few Baptists only. Where is it now? It has long since, as is presumed, been lost. Nor have the modern Baptists of Virginia done much better. Who among them has even attempted, in any form, to "rebut the calumnies of Dr. Hawks, of Dr. Foote, of Dr. Alexander, or of Bishop Meade?" Not one. Ought the Fathers to have thus left these unmerited reproaches, and injurious misrepresentations uncontradicted and unexposed? What can he do for the cause of truth and salvation, in whose intelligence, honor, and integrity, the public have ceased to repose entire confidence? Their duty to Christ demanded an ample and adequate defence. But they were almost entirely silent, and permitted all these reproaches to float into the current of literature, and from the in-

* History of the Virginia Baptists, p. 88.

12

juries thus inflicted, the Baptist churches of our country have until the present hour not entirely recovered.

5. The Early Baptists of Virginia, committed a serious error in their failures to plant churches in the cities and other important centres of influence in the commonwealth.

These centres of influence are like the fortresses and strongholds of a country. The party that possesses them exerts over the whole nation a power hard to be successfully resisted. Gloriously did they establish the truth throughout the country. To the cities they gave very little attention. Successfully to have cultivated them, would have required much policy and management, and they were not, in these respects especially, men of policy and management. They preached when and where God's blessing upon their efforts seemed to them for the moment most rich and abundant. These centres of influence were probably not very highly appreciated by them. However this might have been, they were left to the occupancy of other denominations, who were more patient and far-sighted than themselves. The various Pedobaptist churches industriously availed themselves of the opportunity to occupy them nearly all, and at the expense of the Baptists. Hardly yet have they obtained in them a position equal to that of their Pedobaptist neighbors.

6. The Early Baptists of Virginia, were also mistaken as to the extent in which unassisted truth will take care of itself.

The correctness of their principles they never doubted. That they must by their own inherent force very soon triumph, they felt an unwavering assurance. They failed to consider the powerful influences constantly operating to counteract and destroy them. They could not understand how any sincere lover of Christ, with the Bible in his hand, could seriously oppose these principles. They were themselves unsophisticated, honest men. They seem to have suspected no one of sinister motives, or ambitious designs. They abjured, therefore, all management and all indirectness. They consequently often found their designs thwarted and defeated; the truth lying wounded and crushed; and error in its most brazen form proudly triumphant. They did not give to truth all the necessary supports which its permanent triumph demanded.

7. Injury to the Baptist churches also resulted from their carelessness in regard to the qualifications of their ministers.

They with propriety refused to demand, as necessary to their ordination, any specified amount of literary and scientific culture. Profound knowledge of the word of God may exist associated with very limited attainments in human learning. Not a few men thus characterized, are much more useful as ministers, than are many of the classically trained. Learning of itself cannot make a minister of even a truly Christian man. He must have the native mind and powers— what the fathers so aptly called "the gifts"—essential to success. Cultivation in literature, the sciences, and the arts is always highly desirable, but not always essential.   In these respects, the fathers judged and acted wisely.   In some important instances, however, they seem to have forgotten that fervent zeal, excellent as it is in itself, cannot supply the absence both of mental power and knowledge.   They ordained to the work of the ministry therefore, some men who were, indeed, excellent, earnest, devoted, self-sacrificing Christians, but wholly unqualified to perform the high duties assigned them.   The intelligent and thoughtful among the churches knew how to apologize for the weaknesses and failures of these preachers, but the masses, and especially of their congregations, were scandalized and repelled.   Through this means, the cause of Christ among them suffered serious and lasting injury.

8. The Early Baptists of Virginia failed to supply the people with suitable books for their instruction.

They preached and prayed and labored with indefatigable industry.   They taught the people daily and from house to house, verbally; but they left with them no books to second their instructions ; nor did they place any of a suitable character within their reach. Of this neglect, the Pedobaptists promptly availed themselves, and distributed liberally, everywhere, their denominational literature.   In this way the force of Baptist teaching was painfully abated, and the minds of thousands were permanently perverted, and turned aside from the truth.   Of these facts, the fathers themselves were not entirely oblivious.   The subject was brought to the attention of the General Association on various occasions.   During the Anniversary held in May, 1800, the General Meeting of Correspondence was charged with the duty of moving in the premises. The plan it devised, but did not execute, was thus substantially sketched by Dr. Semple :*

"They were instructed to collect and publish useful pieces, somewhat in the form of a Magazine, and sell it to defray its expenses."

This enterprise, so praiseworthy in its inception, was probably never commenced. At subsequent sessions some valuable books were distributed, and others were recommended for publication. Here the whole matter rested. Pedobaptist books flowed into all the channels of circulation. Besides the Bible, Baptists distributed almost no others. Had they then gone actively into the business of publication and colportage, as they did fifty years afterwards, how great the blessing they would have conferred upon the world generally, and the Baptist churches especially!

These mainly, were the evils which had their origin among the Early Baptists of Virginia, and which have since so sorely afflicted the churches; the Baptists failed to take their part in the education of the people; they mistook the true relation between religion and the use of money, as a means of its advancement; the manner in which certain classes of their members were accustomed to express themselves in society, in regard to the churches generally, and the ministers especially; their carelessness in defending the honor of their churches and people; their neglect to plant churches in the cities and other important centres of influence in the commonwealth; their mis-

---

* History of the Virginia Baptists, p. 87.

take as to the extent to which unassisted truth will take care of itself; their carelessness in regard to the qualifications of their ministers for the work assigned them; and their failure to supply the people with suitable books for their instruction. These errors were all most unhappy in themselves, and in their consequences. Of their nature and extent, it is hoped the people are now fully aware. Much has been done to correct them, and by the blessing of God, they will, it is believed, be effectually surmounted. No one can doubt, however, that through their influence the churches are at this moment far inferior in numbers, influence, and usefulness, to what they might have been under an administration more wise and judicious.

CHAPTER XI.

POLITICAL ACTION OF THE BAPTIST GENERAL ASSO-
CIATION.

Design of the General Association of Virginia. Its declaration of principles on political subjects. Principles of the primitive Christians. Of the English Baptists. Its memorials to the Convention and Legislature. Memorials of the other denominations. Its commissioners. Baptist principles embodied in the Virginia Constitution.

THE General Association of the Baptists of Virginia, as we have seen in a former chapter, was an organization designed mainly for political purposes, and to be temporary in its continuance. It entered, therefore, fully—as did the General Committee of Correspondence by which it was superceded, and the General Meeting of Correspondence into which that was finally merged—into all the State questions of the day, and with great zeal and effect into all those which had any bearing upon the religious rights of the people. These questions were regularly brought before them at their Annual Meetings, carefully canvassed, their decisions recorded, and their commissioners appointed to attend the Legislature, represent their views to its members, and, if possible, secure their adoption by that body. A similar course was pursued by the other denominations, but they acted regularly through their established church organizations. The Baptists found it necessary to institute a new body, through which to concentrate their energies, and bring their influence to bear upon the government of the State.

During the first three years of its existence, its proceedings of a political character, had reference mainly to the persecutions waged against the Baptists by the Colonial rulers, under the pressure of the State Church party. Measures were proposed in the General Association, discussed publicly, and at length adopted, and afterwards carried rigorously into effect, to assist their imprisoned and suffering brethren; days of fasting and prayer were appointed and devoutly observed; and the brethren were solicited to offer constant prayers to God, that he would be merciful to their "poor blind persecutors," and deliver his people from the religious and political thraldom in which they were then so painfully bound. All classes of Baptists, since they all suffered together, were represented in the General Association, and all became intensely interested. We have before seen how much these considerations had to do in inducing that body to seek their full and permanent reunion, and in achieving this most happy result.

The session of the General Association of 1774 was that which committed itself to the doctrine of Episcopacy, which in the eighth chapter of this work has been described with sufficient particularity.

Time wore on. The controversy of the Colonies with the Mother Country, which had been so long rising, now grew rapidly warmer and more intense. It had almost reached its utmost height. Virginia, especially, was heaving like a volcano, whose pent-up fires it was evident could not much longer be repressed. Measures had been adopted by the authority of the Colony, to assemble a Convention to consider the state of the country generally, and of Virginia particularly; and devise, if practicable, some effectual means for their defence and safety. These were the circumstances, religious and political, under which the General Association assembled in 1775. The meeting was held at Manokin Town, and commenced its session on the fourth Saturday in May. Sixty *churches* were in attendance by their messengers, besides the delegations from the various District *Associations.* The assembly was immense in numbers, and characterized by the presence of extraordinary talents. Such men were in attendance as Harris and Metcalf, Lovell and Hargitt, Maneese and Chastaine, Johnston and Walker, Ellington and ·Williams, Childs, Thompson, Tribble, Waller, Burruss, Ford, Twyman, Bennett, Eve, Munroe, Peyton, Holtsclaugh, Winters, Marshall, Pickett, and many others of like reputation and abilities.

After the painful agitations arising in this session from the doctrinal discussions, of which we had occasion to speak in the seventh chapter of this work, and the happy union to which they led, the General Association proceeded to consider what would be proper to be done by them in the existing political crisis of the country. They decided to embody their opinions and desires in an address to be presented to the State Convention, then soon to assemble in Richmond. A committee, the names and number of which are not recorded, was appointed and charged with the duty of preparing the proposed address. After completing the other business of the session, the General Association adjourned to meet again at Du Puy's, in Cumberland, now Powhattan County, on the second Saturday in August, to give the Committee time to accomplish the work assigned it.

The General Association assembled at the time and place appointed. The committee reported the address, which was carefully canvassed, and after a deliberation of two days, unanimously adopted. Rev. Messrs. Jeremiah Walker, John Williams, and George Roberts, were appointed commissioners on the part of the Baptists of Virginia to present their address to the Convention; and these gentlemen were especially instructed to remain at the Capitol during the session, to mingle and converse freely with the members of the Convention, and to employ every honorable means to attain the ends proposed.

These two sessions of the General Association were, in their character and results, as subsequent events have shown, among the most important meetings which have ever been held by any Christian people since the days of the Apostles. Their movement was precisely at the most favorable moment, and was fully and wholly in the proper direction. Referring to the circumstances of the times and the spirit of the churches and people, Dr. Semple remarks:*

"The discontents in America, arising from British oppression, were drawing to a crisis." "This was a very favorable season for the Baptists. Having been

* History of the Virginia Baptists, p. 62.

much ground under British laws," "they were, to a man, favorable to any revolution by which they could obtain freedom of religion."

The address, which was adopted, and which was filed among the State papers of Virginia, contemplated two objects: the freedom of the colony from British rule, and the freedom of religion from all government trammels and direction. The former of these objects is thus noticed in the journals of the Convention:

"An address from the Baptists of this colony was presented and read, setting forth that, however distinguished from their countrymen by appellations and sentiments of a religious nature, they nevertheless considered themselves as members of the same community in respect to matters of a civil nature, and embarked in the same common cause; that alarmed at the oppression which hangs over America, they had considered what part it would be proper for them to take in the unhappy contest, and had determined that in some cases it is lawful to go to war; and that we ought to make a military resistance to Great Britain in her unjust invasion, tyrannical oppression, and repeated hostilities; that their brethren had liberty at discretion to enlist [in the service of the country] without incurring the censure of their religious community; and that, under the circumstances, many had enlisted as soldiers; and that many more were ready to join the army;" "that their ministers would encourage the young men of their churches and congregations to enter the service; and that they asked for themselves permission to serve the army in the capacity of Chaplains."*

* Journal of the Convention, p. 17.

These representations show that the Baptists were in the van of the American patriots of those days. Not all, even of the leaders of the people, were as yet ready to break with England. They were anxious to secure their rights and obtain for their preservation satisfactory guaranties; but they believed that this could be done without forfeiting the protection of the British crown, which they wished to retain, or incurring a war, the issue of which they feared might not be favorable to the colonies. "The Baptists, to a man, were in favor of revolution." The Convention, as is well known, ultimately instructed the delegates in the Colonial Congress to vote for the Declaration of American Independence. Upon this act, Virginia patriotism has ever prided itself. The Baptists, as a body, and unanimously, had long before taken the same position now assumed by the Convention. To what extent the Convention was moved to that gallant proceeding by the Baptist address, and the presence and constant exhortations of their able commissioners, is an inquiry which every man will decide for himself. If, however, this great action reflected honor upon the Convention, the same action previously taken by the Baptists reflects still higher honor upon them; and it becomes exalted and noble when it is remembered, that they urged it upon the Convention as a duty which it owed, not to Virginia only, but to the whole nation.

The second object sought in this address of the General Association of Virginia was "Religious Freedom," not alone for themselves, but also for the whole people. As an expression of their views on this subject, they embodied in their address a formal Declaration of the Principles they held, and which had been maintained by Baptists in all ages. We copy the following extract:

" We hold that the mere toleration of religion by the civil government is not sufficient; that no State Religious Establishment ought to exist; that all religious denominations ought to stand upon the same footing; and that to all alike the protection of the Government should be extended, securing to them the peaceable enjoyment of their own religious principles and modes of worship."*

How slow have men been in all·ages to learn the truths here so explicitly stated! How difficult it has been for them to perceive the difference between *religious toleration* and *religious freedom!* How prone to confound them together, and regard them as substantially the same! The two are, indeed, far asunder as the poles. Toleration, in its best form, is essentially partial and unjust. Freedom is just, generous, beneficent. Toleration implies a privilege granted by a superior to an inferior party. It contains within itself an assertion of the right to withdraw it at pleasure, and therefore the right to persecute dissenters from the religion of the stronger party. The acceptance of toleration is a confession that Government may dictate the religion of the governed, and has the right to enforce its demands in that behalf, since the power which has the right to make a law has also the right to execute its provisions and punish its infractions. Religious

* Semple's History of the Virginia Baptists, p. 62.

13

freedom is altogether of another character. It is a right which God gives to every man; it is prior to all human governments, and beyond their control; it is inalienable; it cannot be abridged nor withdrawn by thrones, by hierarchies, nor by legislatures. The principles of religious freedom were announced nearly nineteen centuries ago by Jesus himself, when he said to the Jews: "Render, therefore, unto Cæsar the things which are Cæsar's, and unto God the things that are God's." They were understood by the Christians of the third century, and were embodied in the Memorial they presented to Constantine the Great on his accession to the throne of the Roman Empire. They petitioned, as affirmed by Eusebius, not for toleration, but for absolute religious freedom for themselves and for all other men of whatever creed. That Emperor readily granted their prayer, and issued "An Ordinance" in which he said:

"As we long since perceived that *Religious Liberty* should not be denied, but that it should be granted to the opinions and wishes of each one to perform divine duties according to his own determination, we had given orders that each one, and the Christians among the rest, have the liberty to observe the religion of his choice, and his peculiar mode of worship." "We have resolved, among the first things, to ordain those matters by which reverence and worship to the Deity might be exhibited; that is, how we may grant likewise to the Christians, and to all, the free choice to follow that mode of worship which they may wish." *

* Cruise's Eusebius, p. 426.

The principles of religious liberty shine forth re-
splendently in the memorable Protest of the Donatists,
"Quid est imperatori cum ecclesia." The doctrines of
Arnold of Brescia on that subject, who was the "avant
courier" of the Reformation, were truly worthy of that
great man. These principles inscribe condemnation
upon the creeds of Luther, of Calvin, of Zwingle, and
of Bucer, every one of which gives the civil magistrate
coercive power in religion. They clothe with honor
the German Anabaptists of 1560, and make distinguished the names of Helwysse, of Bunyan, and of
Roger Williams. But in America they were first, since
the days of Constantine, successfully asserted; and its
oral advocates, its *meropes anthropoi*, stood forth gloriously in Virginia.

The doctrines on political subjects, held by the Baptists of Virginia, and set forth in their address to the
State Convention, may be summarily stated thus: 1.
That religion should be free absolutely, in its doctrines
and ordinances, from any restraints whatever, imposed
by the civil power; 2. That the State Religious Establishment should, as such, be discontinued, and, as an
organization supported by the government, exist no
more; 3. That no favor should be shown by the State
to one religious denomination more than to another;
4. That all should receive alike the protection of the
civil government in the full exercise of all their rights.

These principles they defended in subsequent memorials, with extraordinary ability and conclusiveness.
In one of them, for example, they said:

"We hold it as a fundamental and indubitable truth,

that the religion of every man must be left to the conviction and conscience of every man, and that it is the right of every man to exercise it as these may dictate. This right in its nature is an *inalienable* right. It is inalienable, because what is here a right towards man is a duty towards the Creator. It is the duty of every man to render to the Creator such homage, and such only, as he believes to be acceptable to him. This duty is precedent, both in order of time and in degree of obligation, to the claims of civil society. Before any man can be considered as a member of civil society, he must be considered as a subject of the Governor of the universe. And if a member of civil society, who enters into any subordinate association, must always do it with a reservation of his duty to the general authority, much more must every man who becomes a member of any particular civil society, do it with a reservation of his allegiance to the Universal Sovereign. We maintain, therefore, that in matters of religion no man's right is abridged by the institution of civil society, and that religion is wholly exempt from its cognizance."

Plainly, "If religion be exempt," as it must be conceded that it is, " from the authority of society at large, still less can it be subject to the authority of the legislative body. The legislative body is the creature and vicegerent of society at large. The jurisdiction of that body is both derivative and limited." It is derived from the will of the people it is chosen to represent, and "it is limited" by the extent of the authority which the people have conferred upon it. If it is limited "with regard to the co-ordinate departments, much more necessarily is it limited with regard to the constituents." The creation and "preservation of a free government require not merely that the metes and bounds which separate each department of power, be invariably maintained, but more especially that neither of them be suffered to overleap the great barrier which defends the rights of the people. The rulers who are guilty of such an encroachment exceed the commission from which they derive their authority, and are tyrants. The people who submit to it are governed by laws made neither by themselves, nor by any authority derived from them, and are slaves."

"All are to be considered as entiring into society on equal conditions; as relinquishing no more, and therefore retaining no less, one than another, of their natural rights; above all are they to be considered as retaining an equal title to the free exercise of religion according to the dictates of conscience. While, therefore, we assert for ourselves a freedom to embrace, to profess, and to observe the religion which we believe to be of divine origin, we cannot deny an equal right to those whose minds have not yet yielded to the evidence which has convinced us. If this freedom be abused, it is an offence against God, not against man. To God, therefore, and not to man, must an account be rendered."

An established religion "implies either that the civil magistrate is a competent judge of religious truths, or that he may employ religion as an engine of civil policy. The former is an arrogant pretension, falsified by facts in all ages, and throughout the world; and the latter is an unhallowed perversion of the means of salvation."*

Such was the address of the General Association of 1775, to the Convention of the State. It demanded full religious freedom, and sustained its demand by conclusive arguments, Scriptural, historical, and logical; it urged upon the Convention the duty of opposing an armed resistance to the usurpations of the British government, and attempting the achievement of the political freedom of the country; it declared the readiness of all its young men to enter the army as soldiers of liberty; and asked for its ministers permission to go with their flocks as chaplains in the army. This was the attitude of the Baptists.

The other denominations also addressed the Convention; the Presbyterians, the Methodists, and the Episcopal Church. Of the Presbyterian petitions, Dr. Foote, the historian of that Church in Virginia, and a distinguished minister of that denomination, observes:

"They were for an ill-defined liberty of conscience, and the disseverance of religion from the civil power. That something ought to be done for dissenters was evident, but what should actually be done was matter of contention." †

The members of that church were slow in acquiring first ideas of religious freedom. Nor was this surprising, when we consider their antecedents at Geneva and in Scotland. At that period they were a small but in-

* Semple's History of the Virginia Baptists, pp. 345, et seq.
† Sketches of Va., p. 323.

fluential denomination in Virginia. Their settlements were commenced before the middle of the eighteenth century. Their churches were composed mainly of a class of persons known as "Scotch Irish," and immigrants from Scotland. At first they were located for the most part "among the hills on the western side of the Blue Ridge." When the revolution commenced, however, they had spread themselves through nearly all the counties of the Commonwealth. The Hanover Presbytery, which had its designation from the county of that name, in which resided Mr. Davies, their most distinguished preacher, had successively, for two years previously, petitioned the Colonial Legislature for what Dr. Foote called "An ill-defined liberty of conscience." Their addresses had reference principally to the predominance of the Episcopal Church, from whose rule they desired to be freed. In regard to the conflict then commencing with England, they said little. To their minds it was of dubious result. Unhappily, they, to say the least, appeared unwilling to assume a position from which, should the country fail to achieve its liberty, they could not readily and safely recede.

The Methodist Church, which had then but lately commenced its career in Virginia, was very strongly opposed, as we shall hereafter see more fully, to all legal reforms, and joined heartily the Episcopal Church in all its struggles to retain its position as the Established Church of the colony, and to defeat the Baptist movement for the attainment of religious freedom.

Such were the positions on this subject of the several

religious denominations before the Convention. For the bold purpose of establishing religious freedom, whether it involved honor or dishonor, deliverance or chains, life or death, the Baptists, and the Baptists alone, were then held responsible by all others, and they held themselves responsible. We have before seen, that for these same doctrines and principles they had for a thousand years been denounced in the Old World by every other church and by every government. They had ever been held as heretics, and the enemies of all political governments, and they had paid with their lives for their daring presumption. In Virginia they were undismayed, and, believing that their circumstances were now favorable for success, determined to put forth all their strength. Two of these circumstances ought here to be mentioned.

The former of these is thus referred to by Rev. Dr. Hawks. He says: "The storm which had so long been gathering burst upon America, and the first blood was spilled at Lexington. Every Colony was speedily on the alert, and a voluntary Convention of the delegates to the Virginia Legislature, meeting after its adjournment, succeeded the Royal Assembly that was held in the 'Ancient Dominion.' The Baptists were not slow in discovering the advantageous position in which the political troubles of the country had placed them. Their numerical strength was such as to make it important to both parties to secure their influence; they knew this, and therefore determined to turn the circumstance to their profit as a sect. Persecution had taught them not to love the Establishment, and they

now saw before them a reasonable prospect of over-
turning it entirely. In their Association they had
calmly discussed the matter, and resolved on their
course; in this course they were consistent to the end.
Now [in the Convention] commenced the assault. Inspired with a patriotism which accorded with their interest; or willing to avail themselves of a favorable
opportunity to present their case in an advantageous
contrast to a part of the Church; they addressed the
Convention, and informed that body that their religious tenets presented no obstacle to their taking up
arms and fighting for their country; and they tendered
the services of their pastors in promoting the enlistment
of the youth of their religious persuasion. They presented also to the Convention a petition, in which they
made the certainly reasonable request, that they might
be allowed to worship God in their own way, without
interruption; that they might be permitted to maintain
their own ministers separate from others; that they
might be married, and buried, and the like, without
paying the clergy of other denominations." He adds,
"A complimentary answer was returned to their [the
Baptists'] address, [by the Convention] and an order
was made that the sectarian clergy should have the
privilege of performing divine service in the army,
equally with the regular chaplains of the Established
Church." He closes this notice by saying, "This, it
is believed, was the first step made towards placing the
clergy of all denominations upon an equal footing in
Virginia." *

* History of the Prot. Epis. Church in Va., pp. 137, 138.

We do not pause to comment on the disrespectful language which the writer used towards the Baptists, his sneers at their patriotism, his ridicule of their privations, nor his charges against them of selfishness, malignity, and sectarian management. All this may pass unnoticed. It is enough that he admits as true all that we have claimed regarding their movements. We will simply add the order to which he refers, as it stands recorded on the Journal of the Convention. It is dated Wednesday, August 16th, 1775, and is as follows:

"*Resolved*, That it be an instruction to the commanding officers of the regiment or troops to be raised, that they permit dissenting clergymen to celebrate divine worship, and to preach to the soldiers, or exhort from time to time, as the various operations of the military service may permit, for the ease of such scrupulous consciences as may not choose to attend divine service as celebrated by the [Episcopal] chaplain."

The other of these favorable circumstances, was found in the character and influence of those members of the Convention who were enlisted in the cause of the Baptists, by the indefatigable exertions of Messrs. Walker, Williams, and Roberts, the Commissioners of the General Association. They soon became intimately associated with Thomas Jefferson, James Madison, and Patrick Henry, all of whom, except the last, entered fully into their spirit and designs. In what respects Mr. Henry failed to sustain the principles of the Baptists, will sufficiently appear in a future chapter. The co-operation and advocacy of these great men, was a very happy event, and led to the most triumphant success. The address of the General Association was read. It was heard with the profoundest attention. The effect was extraordinary. An impression was made, which no counter influences could ever subsequently efface, and which, with the blessing of God, became continually deeper and broader, until in every sense Virginia was free.

The action of the Convention of Virginia was equally gratifying and complimentary to the Baptists of the Commonwealth. The General Association urged the Convention to oppose an armed resistance to the usurpation of England, and pledged, to support it in that opposition, all its men and all its wealth; and the Convention instructed its delegates in Congress to declare the independence of the Colonies, and to pledge for its support their lives, their fortunes, and their sacred honor. It asked for its ministers the privilege of serving as chaplains in the army of liberty; and by order of the Convention the commanding officers were instructed to receive them on the same footing with the chaplains of the Established Church. It maintained in its address that no State Establishment ought to exist; that all religious denominations in the State ought to stand upon the same footing; that to all alike should be extended its protection, securing to them the peaceable enjoyment of their own religious principles and modes of worship; and that these grand principles ought to be embodied in the organic law of the Commonwealth. The Convention formed a constitution for the State. The first Article in the Bill of Rights, adopted June 12th, 1776, asserts, accordingly, that "all men are by nature equally free and independent;" and the sixteenth Article of the Constitution maintains that "religion, or the duty which we owe to our Creator, and the manner of discharging it, can be directed only by reason and conviction, not by force or violence, and therefore all men are equally entitled to the free exercise of religion according to the dictates of conscience; and it is the mutual duty of all to practice Christian forbearance, love, and charity towards each other." Consequently, the religion of the citizen cannot be the subject of legislation, nor render him amenable to the civil magistrate. If he abuse religious freedom, it is an offence, not against men, but against God. To God only, therefore, can he be justly called to account.

So great and extraordinary is this victory, achieved in legislation by the Baptists of Virginia, that it seems almost incredible. Yet there stands the monument which affirms it. These grand principles were up to that time known to be peculiarly Baptist, and denounced by all others. We need not inquire whether they had converted to their political sentiments a majority of the members of the Convention before the assembling of that body, or whether after their meeting they were induced to adopt them. In either case the result is the same. A summary of Baptist principles was embedded in the Constitution of the State, and thus placed immovably at the very foundation of the government. It was a glorious triumph. Such was its character as almost certainly to secure success in every subsequent conflict.

CHAPTER XII.

INFLUENCE OF THE BAPTISTS IN FORMING THE
STATE GOVERNMENT OF VIRGINIA.

*Petitions to the Virginia Legislature from the General Association.
From the Hanover Presbytery, and other Presbyteries. Methodist
petitions. Episcopal claims. Jefferson's advocacy of Baptist principles Marriage law. Assessment law. Law to establish religious
liberty. Suspension of the salaries before paid by the State to the
established clergy. The Vestry and Glebe laws.*

" THE share which the Baptists took in shoring up
the fallen liberties of England, and in infusing new
vigor and liberality into the constitution of that country," says Rev. Dr. W. R. Williams, referring to the
times of Cromwell, " is not generally acknowledged.
It is scarcely even known. The dominant party in
the Church, and in the State, at the Restoration, became the historians. And when 'The man, and not
the lion was the painter,' it was easy to foretell with
what party all the virtues, all the talents, and all the
triumphs would be found. When our principles shall
have won their way to a more general acceptance, the
share of the Baptists in the achievements of that day
will be disinterred, like many other forgotten truths,
from the ruins of history. Then it will be found, we
believe, that while dross, such as has alloyed the purest
churches, in the best ages, may have existed in our
denomination, yet the body was composed of pure and
scriptural Christians, who contended manfully, with

14

some bitter sufferings, for the rights of conscience, and the truth as it is in Jesus; that to them English liberty owes a debt it can never acknowledge; and that amongst them Christian freedom found its earliest, and some of its staunchest, its most consistent, and its most disinterested champions." * These representations of the Baptists of England are peculiarly applicable to the Baptists of Virginia. The historians of the State were not their friends; some of them were their traducers; and by all of them they have been studiously ignored as far as literary decency would permit. It is only when we go back to the facts, actions, and records, of the times, and investigate for ourselves the original sources of knowledge, that we find everywhere prominently inscribed their patriotic deeds, and their noble achievements. They were ever ready to "Render unto Cæsar the things which are Cæsar's;" but their souls were too free and too determined, not to resist Cæsar when he demanded from them also, "the things that are God's." They seized, therefore, this favorable opportunity—such an opportunity as had never before occurred, and probably would never occur again—to fix their political principles in the government of the State and of the country. They had succeeded in planting their doctrine in the Constitution; by this fact they were greatly encouraged; they determined to redouble their exertions; and never to cease their agitations, until they had overthrown the State Religious Establishment, and procured the enactment of such laws as would give all the people full religious liberty.

* Benedict's History of the Baptists, pp. 322, et seq.

The session of the General Association of the Baptists of Virginia for 1776 was characterized by peculiar proceedings, some of which have been narrated. At that meeting occurred the election and ordination of the first Baptist Diocesan Bishop of Virginia. But it did not forget its duty to the government and to its constituents. Its Commissioners to the State Convention, Mr. Walker, Mr. Williams, and Mr. Roberts, reported, giving a full account of their mission, and the extraordinary success with which God had crowned their endeavors. They received the grateful thanks and earnest congratulations of all their brethren.

An address to the Legislature soon to convene was reported, considered, and adopted. This paper I have been unable to find. We are, however, not without information as to its contents, contained in the Journals of the Legislature, and the current history of the times. From these sources we learn that the Baptists followed up, with characteristic energy, the measures they had previously devised. The Legislature was convened in October. "It was addressed," says Dr. Hawks,* "by numerous petitions from all parts of the State, entreating for all religious sects protection in the full exercise of their several modes of worship, and exemption from the payment of all taxes for the support of any church whatever, further than what might be agreeable to their own private choice or voluntary obligation." Prominent among these petitioners was the Hanover Presbytery, to which we have before referred. This body was led by Patrick Henry, who lived in Hanover County,

* Hist. Prot. Epis. Ch. in Va., p. 139.

and though not a communicant in that body, was of Presbyterian antecedents, his father being a Scotchman, and of that church. Over the minds of both the ministers and members of that denomination in Virginia, Mr. Henry exercised, on political subjects, an almost unlimited influence. These Presbyterian petitions are characterized, as we have seen, by Dr. Foote, their able historian, as indefinite, "ill-defined," and left only the impression "that something ought to be done for dissenters;" "but as to what should be done," they were not agreed among themselves. The address of the Methodist Church is sufficiently characterized by the reference to it upon the Journal of the House of Delegates. It is dated Monday, October 27th, 1776, and is as follows:

"A petition from the people commonly called Methodists was presented to the house and read; setting forth that the Dissenters are preparing to lay a petition before the House for abolishing the present Establishment of the Church; and as they may, also, in the opinion of some, come under the denomination of Dissenters, they beg leave to declare, that they are a society in communion with the Church of England, and do all in their power to strengthen and support said Church; and as they conceive very bad consequences will arise from the abolishing the Establishment, they therefore pray that the Church of England, as it ever hath been, may continue to be the Established Church."

Referring to the petitions of the Baptists and Presbyterians, Dr. Hawks of the Episcopal Church says: "Counter memorials on the part of the Church [Episcopal] and the Methodists solicited the continuance of the Establishment." "They claimed this upon the principles of justice, of wisdom, and of policy."* They insisted "that the efforts made [by the sects] to injure what was left of the Establishment might be checked" by the legislative authority.†

The Baptist address was not indefinite, ambiguous, nor compromising. Dr. Hawks says: "It entreated for all religious sects protection in the full exercise of their several modes of worship and exemption from the payment of all taxes for the support of any church whatever." He adds: "*Further* than what might be agreeable to their own private choice or voluntary obligation." This last statement was true of the Presbyterians, but, as is well known, not true of the Baptists. If the Presbyterians were unwilling to be *taxed by the State* "for the support of any church whatever *further* than what might be *agreeable to their own private choice*," the Baptists were unwilling to be taxed by *the State* for the support of any church whatever; even for that of "their own private choice." They preferred to support it in their own way, and denied that the State had a right to interfere in any of their affairs, or even to inquire into such matters. They insisted that any Religious Establishment by the State was in its very nature impolitic, unjust, and oppressive, and that none could exist compatibly with religious freedom.

In accordance with these views a bill was brought into the Legislature to "Repeal all laws establishing

* Hist. Prot. Ep. Ch. in Va., p. 142.
† Idem, p. 147.

the Episcopal Church," as the State Church of Virginia. The introduction of this bill produced immense excitement, and its progress was strenuously contested at every step. Amendments were proposed and adopted, until it assumed quite another form, and fell far short of its original object. It did not abolish the Established Church. Still it repealed some most obnoxious laws, which however had been for several years of impracticable execution. In this mutilated form, the law was adopted. It provided as follows :

"Be it enacted by the General Assembly of the Commonwealth of Virginia, and it is hereby enacted by the authority of the same, that all and every Act of Parliament, by whatever title known or distinguished, which renders criminal the maintaining any opinions in matters of religion [other than Episcopal], forbearing to repair to church, or the exercising any mode of worship whatsoever, or which prescribes punishment for the same, shall henceforth be of no validity or force within this Commonwealth." And "That all dissenters of whatever denomination, from the said Church, shall from, and after the passing of this Act, be totally free and exempt from all levies, taxes, and impositions whatever, towards supporting and maintaining said Church."*

Even this inadequate boon was not gained without an arduous and protracted struggle. Mr. Jefferson, in his works,† refers to the conflict it created, in the following terms :

* Hening's Statutes at Large, vol. 9, p. 164.
† Vol. 1, pp. 32, 33.

"·The first Republican Legislature, which met in 1776, was crowded with petitions to abolish this spiritual tyranny. (The Established Church.) These brought on the severest contest in which I have ever been engaged." "The petitions were referred to a Committee of the whole House on the State of the Country; and after desperate contests in that Committee almost daily, from the 11th of October, to the 5th of December, we prevailed so far only as to repeal the laws·which rendered criminal the maintenance of any religious opinions (other than those of the Episcopalians), the forbearance of repairing to (the Episcopal) Church, or the exercise of any (other than the Episcopal) mode of worship ; and to suspend only until the next session, levies on the members of that Church for the salaries of their own incumbents." "Our opponents carried, in the General Resolutions of November the 19th, a declaration that Religious Assemblies ought to be regulated, and that provision ought to be made for continuing the succession of the clergy, and superintending their conduct."

This was the only action of the first Legislature on the subject. Some progress was made, but much less than was hoped. The Establishment was continued, and supported by the State. It was, however, no longer a crime, punishable by the civil magistrate, not to attend an Episcopal Church, or to decline the use of the Episcopal form of worship, and dissenters of all classes were not to be taxed to pay the salaries of the Episcopal clergy, but their "Religious Assemblies," were "to be regulated" by the civil authority.

The session of the General Association of the Baptists of Virginia for 1777, was rendered memorable by a proceeding which clothes that body with immortal honor. A committee was appointed, charged with the duty of examining the laws of the Commonwealth, and designating all such as were justly considered offensive; of recommending the method to be pursued to obtain their removal from the Statute Book; to propose in form such laws, to be laid before the Legislature, as should firmly establish and maintain "Religious freedom," in all its extent and bearings; and to report at the earliest moment practicable. The task assigned this committee was indeed immense; doubtless the necessary materials had been previously prepared for it; the labor was soon accomplished; and in due time it presented an elaborate report. In that report, numerous laws were designated as offensive, prominent among which was the law which required all marriages to be performed by Episcopal clergymen, with the ceremonies of the Established Church, and made all otherwise performed illegal and void; and all the laws establishing the Episcopal Church as the religion of the State, and providing for its support from the public purse; as the best method to procure their removal from the Statute Book, continued agitations among the people, and petitions to the Legislature were recommended; and as expressive of such govenment action, as was desired, a law was drawn up in form, and reported, entitled "An Act for the Establishment of Religious Freedom," to be presented to the Legislature, with an earnest petition that it might be adopted as a law of the State.

This report was received, amply discussed, and adopted. An address was prepared embodying all the suggestions of the report, especially the proposed law to establish Religious Liberty; commissioners were appointed, to whose fidelity it was confided; and they were instructed to remain with the Legislature, and give their attention to these interests during the approaching session.

The General Assembly met, and as in the previous year, "was flooded with petitions." The Baptists, with whom were joined the masses of the people, and who were seconded on some topics by the Presbyterians, were the memorialists on the one side, and on the other were the Episcopalians and Methodists. Very little progress was made. The Assembly again suspended for a year the collection of the taxes levied upon the people, for the support of the Established Church. This, however, was a small affair, since the clergy of that church lived plentifully, and in fine style upon their glebes, and were not wholly dependent upon the extra salary they had heretofore received directly from the Treasury of the State.

Meantime a new theory of a *State Religious Establishment* was devised, and began, in private circles, to be warmly discussed. This theory had its origin with the Presbyterians, and was in their subsequent memorials tenaciously and elaborately advocated. It proposed, not the abrogation of a State Religious Establishment, the measure demanded by the Baptists, but that the State, instead of selecting one denomination, as the Episcopal, and establishing that as the religion of the State, and giving to that alone its support, should establish all the denominations, Presbyterians, Methodists, and Baptists, as well as the Episcopalians, and make them all equally and alike *the religion of the State*, and to be *supported by the State.* How this could be done we shall hereafter see fully explained in some of the Presbyterian memorials. Of this plan of reconciling and harmonizing all parties, Patrick Henry was the ablest and most eloquent advocate. It had the merit of British precedent, since Episcopalianism in England, and Presbyterianism in Scotland, were alike the Established Religion of the Empire. Baptists, and Methodists, and any other strong denomination that might afterwards arise, could easily be added here, without any change in the principle. The plan was ingenious, but it had two great impediments to overcome. The one was the determined tenacity with which the Episcopalians and Methodists clung to the existing Establishment, and the other was the undying hostility of the Baptists to any State Religious Establishment whatever. The proposal to include them in such an Establishment, they scouted with indignation. They demanded the total and perpetual separation of Church and State.

The General Association, at its session in 1778, renewed its vigilance regarding all the interests which the denomination had committed to its charge. A committee of seven members was appointed to consider "Civil Grievances." That committee reported as such

the State Religious Establishment; taxes for its support; the glebes; the marriage law and other laws;
and denounced especially the new Presbyterian device,
which proposed the establishment and support of all denominations as the religion of the State. An address
to the Legislature, embodying these topics, and praying
for the passage of a law "establishing Religious Freedom," was adopted, and placed in the hands of Jeremiah Walker, Elijah Craig, and John Williams, who
were appointed commissioners, with the usual instructions. The country was now in the midst of the war
of the Revolution; the Legislature was wholly engrossed with the measures necessary for its defence; and
for the mitigation of these civil grievances, nothing
was accomplished.

When the General Association assembled in 1779,
Mr. Walker, after having reported the proceedings of
the commissioners at the capital, made to the body a
most important communication. Two years before, a
committee had reported to that body the project of a
law for "the Establishment of Religious Liberty."
This form had been embodied in its memorial, and
submitted to the Legislature. The General Assembly,
as we have seen, was then in no temper to act favorably
on this, or on any similar subject. The form submitted
had, however, attracted the attention of several members of the Legislature, and especially of Mr. Jefferson and Mr. Madison, and had led to various private
interviews between them and the commissioners on the
subject. Mr. Jefferson had kindly undertaken to prepare the law; make it accord with their wishes; render

it as perfect as possible; and at the earliest practicable day secure its adoption by the General Assembly as a law of the State. This form, as thus prepared, was now laid before the General Association by Mr. Walker, for its consideration, advice, and approval. The paper was read carefully, and prayerfully considered, and the following proceedings unanimously adopted:

"*Resolved*, That the [proposed] bill establishing Religious Liberty, in our opinion puts that subject upon its proper basis; preserves the just limits of the powers of the State with regard to religion; and properly guards against partiality towards any religious denomination; and that, therefore, we heartily approve the same, and desire it to pass into a law.

"Ordered that this our approbation of said bill be transmitted to the public printers, that it may be published in the *Gazette*." *

The memorial for this year transmitted by its commissioners to the Legislature the bill referred to, with the statement of its unanimous approval by the General Association, and its prayer that it might be passed into a law; it petitioned for the abolition of the State Religious Establishment; it protested against the new scheme, which proposed the taxing of the people for the support of the ministers of all denominations; and remonstrated against any further payment of the salaries of the Episcopal clergy. Only one of these topics— the last named—engaged the attention of the Assembly. That body adopted an act entitled "An Act to repeal so much of the Act for the support of the clergy,

* Semple's History of the Virginia Baptists, passim.

and for the regular collecting and paying of the parish
levies, as relates to the payment of the salaries heretofore given to the clergy of the Church of England."
The principal provision of this law is as follows:—

"Be it enacted by the General Assembly, That so
much of the act entitled An Act for the support of the
clergy, and for the regular collecting and paying of
the parish levies; and of all and every other act providing salaries for the ministers, and authorizing the
vestries to levy the same; shall be, and the same are
hereby repealed." *

This was a bold and effectual blow. It refused any
longer to pay the ministers of the State Church, but it
still retained it as the State Church!

This law, which Dr. Hawks regards as that which
effectually destroyed the Establishment in Virginia, he
attributes mainly to the influence of the Baptists. That
gentleman, in a strain of lamentation, thus expresses
himself:—

"In each successive meeting of the Legislature from
1776 to 1779, this *questio vexata* was brought up for
discussion, and the friends of voluntary contribution,
apprehensive probably of a final vote against them,
labored, and not without success, to suspend the decision from time to time, and leave the matter to be
debated the succeeding year. In 1779, all things being now ready for a final vote, the question was settled," "and the Church was finally put down." "The
Baptists," he adds, "were the principal promoters of
this work, and in truth aided more than any other de-

* Hening's Statutes at Large, vol. 10, p. 197.

15

nomination in its accomplishment." "In the Associations of that sect, held from year to year, a prominent subject of discussion always was as to the best mode of carrying on the war against the former Establishment. After their final success in this matter [the overthrow of the Establishment] their next efforts were to procuré the sale of the Church lands." *

"The Church lands," of which the author here speaks, were the Virginia "glebes." "The Vestry laws," of which we shall hereafter have frequent occasion to speak more fully, provided that "Twelve of the most able men of each parish be, by the major part of said parish, chosen to be a vestry; out of which number the minister and vestry to make choice of two church wardens yearly; as also in the case of the death of any vestryman, or his departure from the parish, that the said minister and vestry make choice of another in his room." To qualify these gentlemen for office, they were required to take "The Oath of Supremacy," and "Subscribe the Doctrines and Discipline of the Church of England." Among the most important duties the vestrymen were called upon to perform, were to lay the parish levy, and collect and pay over the amount to the minister." †

Properly to understand the value of the "Virginia glebes," and the manner in which they were created and directed, we will refer more at large to the leading enactments on that subject.

* History of the Protestant Episcopal Church in Virginia, pp. 152, 153.

† Laws of Va., Revised folio edition, 1769, pp. 2, 250.

The "law of March 6th, 1655–6," provides "That parishes be laid out in every county;" and that "by a tax upon the people," funds be collected "to purchase [in each parish] a glebe and stock for the minister that shall be settled there."

It was enacted, " March 9th, 1657–8, That further taxes be laid upon the people, for the purchasing of glebes and stock for the ministers."

In 1748 the following law on the subject was enacted:

"That in every parish in this Dominion, where a good and comfortable glebe is not already purchased and appropriated, a good and convenient tract of land, to contain two hundred acres at least, shall be purchased by the vestry, and assigned and set apart for a glebe for the use of the minister of such parish and his successors in all times hereafter; and where a mansion and other convenient outhouses are not already erected for the habitation of the minister, it is hereby declared and enacted, that the vestry of every such parish shall have power, and they are hereby authorized and required, to cause to be erected, and built on such glebe, one convenient mansion house; kitchen; barn; stable; dairy; meat-house; corn-house; garden, well paled, or inclosed with a mud fence; with such other conveniences as they shall think fit; and to levy the charge of the glebe lands and buildings on the titheable persons in their respective parishes." *

Each parish had one of these extensive farms for the use of the Episcopal minister. They were usually

* Laws of Virginia, Revised, Fol. 1769, pp. 250, 251, 252.

among the best farms, and had upon them the handsomest and best houses and other improvements, in the country. Some of these old residences yet remain, and contrast favorably with the finest mansions of modern erection. All this property was purchased with the money of the people, of all the people without distinction of sect; and, therefore, of right belonged to the people. The Baptists maintained that the State Establishment should be abolished, and these estates should be returned to the people, and sold to assist in paying the public debt, the taxes for which purpose were heavy and would thereby be materially lightened. Such were the glebe laws, and the glebes of Virginia.

The General Association of the Baptists of Virginia, assembled in Annual Session in 1780, and passed harmoniously through the usual routine of business. The records of that session that remain, are exceedingly meager, but from contemporaneous history we ascertain that it acted with its accustomed singleness of purpose, vigor, and success. In the Legislature of that year, "The Marriage Law," against which the Baptists and Presbyterians had annually, for several years, earnestly protested in their addresses to the Legislature, was repealed, and another substituted in its place, entitled, "An Act declaring what shall be a lawful Marriage." The chief provisions of this law were as follows:

"That it shall be lawful for any minister of any society or congregation of Christians, to join together as man and wife, those who may apply to him, agreeable to the rules and usages of the respective societies to which the parties to be married, respectively belong."* This law, however, which had been so perseveringly sought, was clogged with various "provisoes," which were of no practical utility, which were exceedingly obnoxious, and which materially abated the satisfaction with which the boon was received by the people. These, however, by the Legislature of 1784, were all removed, and the ministers of all denominations were placed, in this respect, upon a perfectly equal footing.

At the place designated for the meeting of the General Association in 1781, the messengers of sixteen churches assembled. The British troops under Lord Cornwallis then passing through the country, were in the immediate neighborhood. The members present hastily organized, appointed the time and place for the next Annual Meeting, and without transacting any further business adjourned.

The meetings of the General Association for 1782 and for 1783 had a full attendance. The remaining laws of the State, regarded by them as unequal and oppressive, received their elaborate attention. Prominent among these were "The Vestry and Glebe Laws." The project before mentioned of incorporating, or establishing as the religion of the State, all the prevailing denominations, and assessing taxes upon the people to support the ministers of all alike, was now warmly advocated by Presbyterians, Episcopalians, and Methodists, and becoming quite popular. To this scheme, the Baptists still gave the most determined opposition, and sent up against it the most vigorous remonstrances. They

---

* Hening's Statutes at Large, vol. 10, p. 361.

also continued to petition for the adoption of the proposed "Act to Establish Religious Freedom." To bear these addresses to the Legislature and to superintend them before that body, Jeremiah Walker was appointed by the former meeting; and by the latter, Reuben Ford and John Waller. The extraordinary state of the country, however, prevented, on the part of the government, any important action upon these subjects.

The session of 1783 was the last regular meeting of the General Association of the Baptists of Virginia. Many considerations induced the opinion that another form of organization would be as efficient and, to many minds, much less objectionable. A meeting was therefore called, to be held in October of that year, for consultation and final action on that subject. That meeting was very largely attended; and after much and anxious deliberation, the following resolution was unanimously adopted:

"*Resolved,* That our General or Annual Association cease, and that a General Committee be instituted, composed of not more than four delegates from each District Association, to meet annually, to consider matters that may be for the good of the whole society."*

The General Association was then dissolved. It existed no more. The General Committee was organized, and took the place of a body whose character and labors have made an impression upon the whole of North America which time can never efface.

* Semple's History of the Virginia Baptists, p. 68.

CHAPTER XIII. .

CHANGE IN THE POLITICAL REORGANIZATION OF THE EARLY BAPTISTS OF VIRGINIA.

Political and religious condition of the country during the period of the General Association. Cause of the anomalous composition of the Association. Purposes to which it was limited. In what respects it exceeded its limits. The result of union among the churches was the adoption, and also the abandonment, of Episcopacy. The extent of its achievements in its legitimate sphere. Character of the General Committee. Its declaration of principles.

THE General Association of the Baptists of Virginia was, in many respects, an extraordinary body. It was characterized, during its whole period, by an amount of talent, firmness, and energy seldom found in any body, religious or civil. In our day, we see in the political walks of our country no such men as Washington, Hamilton, Jefferson, Franklin, and Madison; and in the religious walks of Virginia, none such appear as Harris, Waller, Williams, Walker, and Craig. That noble body deserves a larger space in Baptist history than it has yet received. Its existence was brief but brilliant, and although it passed in several instances beyond its prescribed limits, and was betrayed into some proceedings which must ever be deprecated, yet its achievements within its proper sphere were numerous, and of the most exalted character. Its motives were always pure; and as to its aberrations, much must be forgiven in consideration of the religious and political agitations, turmoils, and conflicts of the times. Religion and politics were both in chaos, and mingled together in the most perplexing confusion. In reducing both to order, and placing each in its true position, it is wonderful that its mistakes were so few, its errors so readily abandoned, and its success so large and beneficial.

The General Association, of which we now write, was an institution wholly different from that which now prevails among the Baptists of Virginia. This was originated, as we have seen in a former chapter, somewhat at large, for purely political purposes. It was required to direct its attention to three grand points: first, to give the sympathy and assistance of the whole denomination to all those who were persecuted and oppressed by the State Church; secondly, to resist and overcome that oppression, by destroying, if possible, all the subsisting connections between the Church and the State; and, thirdly, to obtain in a legal and permanent form, "full and complete religious freedom." The work assigned it was surely sufficiently Herculean to employ all its powers, without the addition of any other. The present General Association of the Baptists of Virginia stands upon a wholly different basis. It is confined to objects purely religious. Its departments are state missions, foreign missions, domestic missions, the education of ministers, the distribution of the Bible, the creation and fostering of Sunday-schools, and the procurement and diffusion among the people of approved religious books. In one respect they were the same. The former was, and so is the latter, strictly prohibited from any interference whatever in the doctrine, discipline, government, or control of the churches. The former committed in this respect a flagrant violation of its trust, and thereby forfeited its existence. Should the latter ever act in a similar manner, it is hoped that it will meet, promptly and surely, a like end. The latter Association did not immediately succeed the former. A period of forty years elapsed between the dissolution of the one and the organization of the other. These explanations are thought desirable, since at some future time, both being of the same name, these two may possibly be mistaken for the same organization.

In some respects, the composition of the General Association was anomalous in its character. It was made up, partly of messengers from District Associations, and partly of messengers from churches. The Ketocton Association, as we have before seen, occupied originally all that portion of Virginia north of James River. This Association took the initiative in favor of a reunion of all classes of Baptists in Virginia and the Carolinas. Active measures were adopted in 1769, and a letter and messengers were sent to the Sandy Creek Association, which occupied that portion of Virginia west of Petersburg, and south of James River, together with the central and western portions of North and South Carolina. This measure was postponed, as we have seen, by the separation, the next year, of the Sandy Creek into three or four parts, with the view of organizing so many different District Associations. The churches of that body in Virginia were detached to form an Association of their own. In

1771, the General Association was organized within that territory, and all these churches, although previously formed into the Rapid Ann, were received as constituents to that body, and with it they continued to act until 1783, when it was dissolved. Many other churches on the north, as well as the south side of the James, were received, so that in a few years it was composed mostly of direct representatives from churches. Its numbers were immense, and the distances they were required to travel to attend the Annual Meetings, were long and tiresome. This is mentioned by Dr. Semple, as one of the reasons for the dissolution of the General Association. He says:—

"They would probably long before this date have divided into districts, had they not been holden together by apprehensions of oppression from civil government. They could not make head against their powerful and numerous opponents, with any hope of success, unless they were united among themselves. In order to be all of one mind, it was necessary that they all should assemble around one Council Board. For these reasons, the General Association was kept up as long as it was. Finding it, however, wearisome to collect so many from such distant parts," "they determined to hold one more General Association," "to form some plan to keep up a Standing Sentinel for political purposes," "and then to divide into districts." This meeting was held, and the body "divided into four districts; Upper, and Lower Districts, on each side of James River."*

---

* History of the Virginia Baptists, pp. 67, 68.

The General Association assumed the place of the Ketocton in its movement to secure a reunion of all classes of Baptists in Virginia and the other southern provinces; and excellent as were its motives, and happy as were, in some respects, the results, it was, nevertheless, a departure from the limits to which it was confined by the articles of its organization, and to which it was pledged strictly to adhere. Precisely at this point is the greatest danger to be apprehended from all such combinations. The excellence of the object is a strong temptation to exceed the limits of its authority, in order to secure its attainment. Most men feel great reluctance to resist a measure of this kind, since their motives may be misunderstood, and they may bring upon themselves a deprecated odium. One departure of this kind becomes a precedent for another, and there is no longer any limit to the license assumed. The excellence of one object may be admitted by all; another object may be, to many minds, of very doubtful character, yet if a majority can be persuaded to believe it good, this also may be sought; thus all constitutions and laws become ropes of sand; and an organized body, religious or civil, may do anything it may choose at the time to consider good and desirable. To go beyond legitimate authority is always evil, in the cases alike of individuals and of organized bodies, no matter for what object; and the old Scripture principle is infinitely wise, which forbids us to "do evil that good may come."

The object so happily secured by the General Association could, it is believed, have been gained just as

effectually by other means, in the then circumstances
of the country. Regular and Separate Churches were
both alike members of that body, and were associated
on equal terms. Had the District Associations followed
the same course, and had no difference been made in
the church as between the two classes of ministers, or
in their communions between the two classes of members, since they suffered alike from the hands of their
persecutors, and sought together the same religious freedom, differing on no very essential doctrines, they must
soon have melted into one mass. They could not, lov-
ing each other as they did, have long been kept asunder.

From the reunion of these two classes of Baptists,
arose another result, which led the General Association
into a much more flagrant violation of the authority
confided to it, than that which was committed in the
other case. One of these parties, as we have before
seen, was of Episcopal antecedents, and naturally desired to see its opinions adopted and acted upon by the
whole body. The reunion was consummated in 1775.
Agitations on the subject of the Episcopacy immediately became intense. Sermons were preached everywhere, and pamphlets on both sides of the subject were
printed and distributed. In 1776, the General Association, assuming to act for the whole denomination,
adopted Episcopacy, and elected and ordained three
bishops, appointing their dioceses, and sending them
forth into the field! The Association was solemnly
pledged never in any respect to interfere with the government of the churches. Yet by this act, or rather by
this series of actions, it changed the whole system of

Ecclesiastical Polity! It did this not only without authority, but against the strictest prohibition, and without even consulting the churches as such. Happily the churches did not readily surrender their liberties, which thus by a single blow were swept away from them; when time was given them to reflect, they did not cordially welcome these apostles, or bishops; the apostles themselves did not press their claims; and the whole scheme, for want of vitality, became nugatory, and was abandoned, informally, but effectually and finally. Thus narrowly did the denomination escape from destruction. Nothing saved the Baptists at that time but the peculiar interposition of Almighty God.

From that hour the General Association was doomed. The special exigencies of the times continued it in being seven years longer; and in its proper sphere, nobly, firmly, successfully, did it acquit itself. The full achievement of "religious liberty" was reserved for its successor, but its victories were numerous and of the greatest importance. In 1775 the Baptists, through its agency, succeeded in planting their principles on the subject of religious freedom, in the State Constitution of Virginia, adopted by the Convention. The next year, 1776, in alliance with the Presbyterians before the Legislature, they succeeded in obtaining the repeal of all the laws making their absence from the regular services of the Episcopal Church criminal, and also the laws requiring them to pay their proportion for the support of the ministers of the Episcopal Church. With the General Association, at its sessions in 1777, originated the law "For the Establishment of Reli-

16

gious Freedom," adopted several years afterwards by the Legislature. Aided by the Presbyterians, they obtained, in 1779, the repeal of all the laws of the State requiring the payment of taxes for the support of the Established Church; and in 1780 the repeal of the Marriage Law, and the authority for dissenting ministers "to celebrate the rites of matrimony." The details through which they passed in the accomplishment of these results have already been presented. The work for which it was organized was but half done; but its aberrations had been too serious to admit of longer endurance; "a Standing Sentinel on Political Subjects" was devised, and after an active being of twelve years, the General Association of the Baptists of Virginia was dissolved.

The General Committee was organized in 1784, and continued to be the centre of denominational action on political subjects, for fifteen years, when having frequently violated its Constitution in a manner similar to the General Association, it forfeited the confidence of its constituents, and in 1799 was dissolved. Like its predecessor, it assumed to act, and did act, in matters of doctrine, and ecclesiastical discipline, for all the churches. This action had regard mainly to the transactions relative to the re-union already narrated in a previous chapter. The object to which the General Committee was confined, as well as the form of its organization may be stated as follows:

"1. The General Committee shall be composed of delegates, sent from all the District Associations, that desire to correspond with each other.

2. No Association shall be represented in the General Committee by more than four delegates.

3. The Committee thus composed, shall consider all the political grievances of the whole Baptist Society of Virginia, and all references from the District Associations respecting matters which concern the Baptist Society at large.

4. No petition, memorial, or remonstrance shall be presented to the General Assembly, from any Association in connection with the General Committee. All such shall originate with the General Committee."*

Being placed in charge of all those interests previously confided to the General Association, like that body, before entering upon the discharge of its duties, it issued its "Declaration of Principles" with regard to civil government. That Declaration cannot here be presented in full. Its most prominent articles are as follows:

"It is believed to be repugnant to the spirit of the gospel for the Legislature to proceed (make laws) in regard to religion; that no human laws ought to be established for this purpose (its regulation, and pecuniary support) but that, in respect to matters of religion, every person ought to be left entirely free; that the Holy Author of our religion needs no such compulsory measures for the promotion of his cause; that the gospel wants not the feeble arm of man for its support; that it has made, and will through divine power again make its way, against all opposition; and that should the Legislature assume the right of taxing

---

* Benedict's History, &c., vol. 2, p. 59.

the people for the support of the gospel, it will be destructive to religious liberty."*

Henceforward the medium through which the Early Baptists of Virginia acted, was different from the former, but its pledges, its objects, its duties, and the men who directed its movements were the same.

* Semple's History of the Virginia Baptists, p. 71.

CHAPTER XIV.

COMPARATIVE POSITION OF THE EARLY BAPTISTS
OF VIRGINIA.

Proceedings of the General Committee. Survey of the field. Episco-
palians and Methodists against religious freedom. Middle ground
of Presbyterians. Baptist hostility to any connection of religion with
the State Government.

THE first Annual Meeting of the General Committee
of the Baptists' of Virginia was held, commencing
October the 9th, 1784. The state of the country, and
what was yet demanded to secure full religious freedom,
received its elaborate consideration. The Vestry and
Glebe laws; the proposed law for "A General Assessment" of all the people, to support the ministers of all
denominations; and the proposed law for "the Incorporation of all Religious Societies," that is, to place
them all upon the same footing in relation to the State
with the Episcopalians, and make each alike the religion of the State, as Presbyterianism in Scotland and
Episcopacy in England are alike the religion of the
British Empire, were fully discussed. Memorials and
petitions were prepared and adopted, protesting against
them all, and Rev. Reuben Ford was appointed to lay
them before the Legislature, and to superintend in that
body all the interests of the Baptists. The proceedings
of the Legislature, at its session for that year, will best
be seen by the report of Mr. Ford to the next meeting

16*

of the General Committee, which commenced its session August 13th, 1785. Dr. Semple says:

"Mr. Ford reported that, according to the directions given him, he presented their memorials and petitions to the Honorable the General Assembly; that certain amendments were made to the marriage law, which rendered it satisfactory; and that the expected bill for a General Assessment had been introduced, and would have passed into a law, but that when at that stage in which it was called an engrossed bill, their [the Baptists'] friends had succeeded in a motion, that the people might be more fully consulted, to refer it to the next Assembly."

Great excitement now prevailed among the people generally, and the Baptists especially. Four measures of the utmost importance were pending; the Assessment bill; the bill to Incorporate the Several Denominations; the bill for the Declaration of Religious Freedom; and the bill for the Repeal of the Vestry and Glebe laws. A great battle was to be fought on these subjects, which was to decide, perhaps for centuries to come, the relations to religion which would be sustained by the government of Virginia. It is, therefore, proper that we should here pause, carefully survey the field, and ascertain the positions, forces, and objects of the various parties who are to mingle in the conflict.

The Episcopalians and Methodists, always allies, as we have seen, sent up their petitions to the Legislature in favor of the Assessment bill; in favor of the bill to Incorporate the Several Denominations; against the bill to establish Religious Freedom; and against the bill for the Repeal of the Vestry and Glebe laws. These petitions were elaborately drawn, and entered largely into argument on these subjects.

The Presbyterians occupied a middle ground. In their memorial, they objected to the pending bill for the Incorporation of the Several Religious Denominations, or Churches, on the ground that the ministers alone, as the bill then stood, were incorporated; but declared themselves in favor of the bill if it were so amended as to include also in the incorporation the people of their churches; and they advocated assessment, provided it were conducted according to a plan which they themselves proposed. On the other subjects, they said nothing. They spoke as follows on the corporation bill:

"We have understood that a comprehensive incorporating act has been, and is at present, in agitation, whereby ministers of the gospel, as such, of certain descriptions, shall have legal advantages, which are not proposed to be extended to the people at large of every denomination. A proposition has been made by some gentlemen in the House of Delegates, we are told, to extend the grace to us among others, in our professional capacity. If this be so, we are bound to acknowledge with gratitude our obligations to such gentlemen, for their inclination to favor us with the sanction of public authority in the discharge of our duty. But as the scheme of incorporating clergymen, independent of the religious communities to which they belong, is inconsistent with our ideas of propriety, we request the liberty of declining any such solitary honor, should it be again proposed. To form clergymen into a distinct order in the community, and especially where it would be possible for them to have the direction of a considerable public estate by such incorporation, has a tendency to render them independent at length of the churches whose ministers they are; and this has been too often found by experience to produce ignorance, immorality, and neglect of the duties of their station."

After stating various considerations which render religion necessary to the civil order and well-being of society, and the stability and success of political government, they proceed to say:

"It is upon this principle alone, in our opinion, that a legislative body has a right to interfere in religion at all, and of consequence we suppose this interference ought only to extend to the preserving of the public worship of the Deity, and the supporting of institutions for inculcating the great fundamental principles of religion, without which society could not easily exist."

The memorial then discusses the subject of assessment, and speaks as follows:

"Should it be thought necessary at present for the Assembly to exert this right of supporting religion in general, by an assessment on all the people, we would wish it to be done on the most liberal plan." "We therefore earnestly pray that nothing may be done in the case, inconsistent with the proper objects of human legislation, or the Declaration of Rights as published at the Revolution. We hope that the assessment will not be proposed under the idea of supporting religion as a spiritual system, relating to the care of the soul, and preparing it for its future destiny. We hope that no attempt will be made [by the Legislature] to point out Articles of Faith, that are not essential to the preservation of society, or to settle Modes of Worship; or to interfere in the internal government of Religious Communities; or to render the ministers independent of the will of the people whom they serve."

The Presbyterians then proceed to present to the Legislature their own plan of assessment, as follows:—

"1st. Religion as a spiritual system is not to be considered as an object of human legislation, but may in a civil view as preserving the existence and promoting the happiness of society.

2d. That public worship and public periodical instruction to the people be maintained in this view, by a general assessment for this purpose.

3d. That every man, as a good citizen, be obliged to declare himself attached to some religious community, publicly known to profess the belief of one God, his righteous providence, our accountability to him, and a future state of rewards and punishments.

4th. That every citizen should have liberty annually to direct his assessed proportion to such community as he chooses.

5th. That twelve titheables or more, to the amount of a hundred and fifty families, as nearly as local circumstances will permit, shall be incorporated, and exclusively direct the application of the money contributed for their support." *

* Memorial of Hanover Presbytery, 1784, in Foote's Sketches of Virginia, pp. 336–338.

A slight analysis of these papers will show that while the Presbyterians objected to the incorporation of their ministers apart from their churches, and denied the right of the State either to prescribe to them Articles of Faith, or to "meddle with their church government," they maintained authority to incorporate churches, and support religion in general by preserving the public worship of the Deity, and sustaining the institutions for inculcating the great fundamental principles of religion; that public worship and public periodical instruction, provided it were orthodox, should be maintained by the State by a tax upon all the people, levied and collected by the Legislature; and that each man paying taxes should be obliged to declare himself attached to some community professing orthodox religion, and to such community should have liberty annually to direct his assessed proportion of taxes for its support. This is the exact position of the Presbyterians of that day on the proper relations between Church and State and the nature of religious liberty.

The Baptists adhered unwaveringly to their original and time-honored principles embodied in their address to the Convention in 1775. Their memorial had been carefully and elaborately prepared by Mr. Madison, one of the ablest logicians, doubtless, of that or of any other age. It maintained the inherent and inalienable right of all men to free and full liberty of conscience and worship; the injustice and injury of any interference with religion by the government; that such interference was unnecessary for the safety and efficiency of civil government, injurious to public morals, and de-

structive of true religion; and that Virginia owed it
to herself, to truth, to justice, and to mankind, to grant
the prayer of the petitioners. This memorial was
signed, not by Baptists only, but also by multitudes of
the people of all classes. This, like the memorial of
the Presbyterians, is too voluminous to be inserted in
full. We have before copied an extract from it for another purpose; and will now present such other extracts as will place the whole subject in a clear and unmistakable light; premising that it takes into view
not only the particular bill mentioned, but all the
other bills then pending, or in prospect before the Legislature, and especially the bill "Establishing Religious Liberty."

"We the subscribers, citizens of the said Commonwealth, having taken into serious consideration a bill
printed by order of the last session of the General Assembly, entitled A Bill Establishing a Provision for
Teachers of the Christian Religion, and conceiving that
the same, if finally armed with the sanction of the law,
will be a dangerous abuse of power, are bound as
faithful citizens of a free State, to remonstrate against it,
and to declare the reasons by which we are determined."

After sustaining by argument the propositions, that
religious freedom is originally the right of every man;
that this right is not abridged by entering into society;
that it cannot be justly invaded by the Legislature;
that religion is necessarily directed by conviction and
conscience, and cannot, therefore, be subject to the authority of rulers; that religious freedom is consequently
an inalienable right; and that any abuse of it is an of-

fence not against men, but against God, to whom alone, and not to men, they are accountable; they proceed to say :—

"We remonstrate against the said bill, because it is proper to take alarm at the first experiment upon our liberties.

"We hold this prudent jealousy to be one of the noblest characteristics of the late Revolution. The freemen of America did not wait until usurped power had strengthened itself by exercise, and entangled the question in precedents. They saw all the consequences in the principle, and they avoided the consequences by denying the principle. We revere this lesson too much soon to forget it. Who does not see that the same authority which can establish Christianity in exclusion of all other religions, may establish with the same ease any particular sect of Christians in exclusion of all other sects? That the same authority which can force a citizen to contribute three pence only of his property for the support of any one establishment, may force him to conform to any other establishment in all cases whatsoever?

"Because the bill violates that equality which ought to be the basis of every law, and which is the more indispensable in proportion as the validity or expediency of any law is more likely to be impeached.

"As the bill violates equality by subjecting some to peculiar burdens, so it violates the same principle by granting to others peculiar exemptions.

"Because the establishment proposed by the bill is not requisite for the support of the Christian religion."

We do not hesitate "to say that it is a contradiction to the Christian religion itself; for every page of it disavows a dependence upon the powers of this world. It is a contradiction of facts; for it is known that this religion both existed and flourished, not only without the support of human laws, but in spite of every opposition from them; and not only during the period of , miraculous aid, but long after it had been left to its own evidence and the ordinary care of Providence. Nay, it is a contradiction in terms; for a religion not invented by human policy, must have pre-existed and been supported before it was established by human policy. It is, moreover, to weaken, in those who profess this religion, a pious confidence in its innate excellence and the patronage of its Author, and to foster in those who still reject it a suspicion that its friends are too conscious of its fallacies to trust it to its own merits.

"Because experience witnesses that ecclesiastical establishments, instead of maintaining the purity and efficacy of religion, have had the contrary operation.

"During almost fifteen centuries has the legal establishment of religion been on trial. What have been its fruits? More or less, in all places, pride and indolence in the clergy; ignorance and servility in the laity; in both, superstition, bigotry, and persecution. Inquire of the teachers of Christianity for the ages in which it appeared in its greatest lustre. Those of every sect point to the ages prior to its incorporation with the civil policy. Propose a restoration to this primitive state, in which its teachers depended upon the voluntary reward of their flocks. Many of them predict its downfall!

17

On which side ought their testimony to have greatest weight? When for, or when against, their interest?

"Because the establishment in question is not necessary for the support of civil government.

"If it be urged as necessary for the support of civil government only as it is a means of supporting religion, and if it be not necessary for the latter purpose, it cannot be necessary for the former. If religion be not within the cognizance of civil government, how can its legal establishment be said to be necessary to civil government? What influence, in fact, have ecclesiastical establishments had on civil society? In some instances they have been seen to erect a spiritual tyranny on the ruins of the civil authority; in more instances have they been seen upholding the thrones of political tyranny; in no instance have they been seen the guardians of the liberties of the people. Rulers who wished to subvert the public liberty may have found an established clergy convenient auxiliaries. A just government, instituted to secure and perpetuate it, needs them not. Such a government will be best supported by protecting every citizen in the enjoyment of his religion with the same equal hand that protects his person and his property, but neither invading the equal rights of any sect, nor suffering any sect to invade those of another.

"Because the proposed establishment is a departure from the generous policy which, offering an asylum to the persecuted and oppressed of every nation and of every religion, promised a lustre to our country and an accession to the number of our citizens.

" What a melancholy mark is the bill of sudden de-
generacy ! Instead of holding forth an asylum to the
persecuted, it is itself a signal for persecution. It
degrades from the equal rank of citizens those whose
opinions on religion do not bend to the legislative authority. Distant as it may be in its present form from
the Inquisition, it differs from it only in degree. The
one is the first step, the other is the last, in the career
of intolerance. The magnanimous sufferer under the
cruel scourge in foreign regions must view the bill as a
beacon on our coast, warning him to seek some other
haven, where liberty and philanthropy, in their due
extent, may offer a more certain repose from his
troubles.

" Because it will have a like tendency to banish our
citizens.

" The allurements presented by other situations are
every day thinning our number. To superadd a fresh
motive to emigration, by revoking the liberty which
they now enjoy, would be the same species of folly
which has dishonored and depopulated flourishing
kingdoms.

" Because it will destroy that moderation and harmony, which the forbearance of our laws to inter-
meddle with religion has produced among its several
sects.

" Torrents of blood have been spilled in the Old
World, by vain attempts of the secular arm to ex-
tinguish religious discord, by proscribing all differences
of religious opinion. Time has at length revealed the
true remedy. Every relaxation of a narrow and rig-

orous policy, wherever it has been tried, has been found to assuage the disease. The American theatre has exhibited proofs that equal and complete liberty, if it does not wholly eradicate it, sufficiently destroys its malignant influence on the health and prosperity of the State. If, with the salutary effect of this system under our own eyes, we begin to contract the bounds of religious freedom, we know no name that will too severely reproach our folly. At least let warning be taken at the first fruits of the threatened innovation. The very appearance of the bill has transformed the 'Christian forbearance, love, and charity,' which of late mutually prevailed, into animosities and jealousies, which may not soon be appeased. What mischiefs may not be dreaded should this enemy to the public quiet be armed with the force of a law?

"Because the policy of the bill is adverse to the diffusion of the light of Christianity.

"The first wish of those who enjoy this precious gift, ought to be, that it may be imparted to the whole race of mankind. Compare the number of those who have as yet received it, with the number still remaining under the dominion of false religions, and how small is the former! Does the policy of the bill tend to lessen the disproportion? No. It at once discourages those who are strangers to the light of truth from coming into the regions of it, and countenances, by example, nations who continue in darkness, in shutting out those who might carry it to them. Instead of leveling, as far as possible, every obstacle to the victorious progress of truth, the bill with an ignoble and unchristian timidity would circumscribe it with a wall of defence, and give all latitude to the encroachments of error.

"Because attempts to enforce, by legal sanctions acts obnoxious to so great a proportion of the citizens, tend to enervate the laws in general, and to slacken the bands of society.

"If it be difficult to execute any law which is not generally deemed necessary or salutary, what must be the case where it is deemed invalid or dangerous? And what may be the effect of so striking an example of impotence in the government, on its general authority?

"Because a measure of such singular magnitude and delicacy ought not to be imposed, without the clearest evidence that it is called for by a majority of the citizens, and no satisfactory method is yet proposed by which the majority in this case may be determined.

"'The people of the respective counties are requested to signify their opinion respecting the adoption of the bill, to the next Legislature;' but (how? By the opinions of the representatives elected?) The representation must be made equal, before the voice, either of the representatives, or of the counties will be that of the people. Our hope is that neither of the former will, after due consideration, espouse the dangerous principle of the bill. Should the event disappoint us, it will still leave us in full confidence, that a fair appeal to the latter will reverse the sentence against our liberties.

"Because finally, 'The equal right of every citizen, to the free exercise of his religion, according to the dictates of conscience,' is held by the same tenure with all our other rights.*

"If we recur to its origin, it is equally (with all our other rights) the gift of nature; if we weigh its importance, it cannot be less dear to us; if we consult the 'Declaration of Rights, which pertain to the good people of Virginia, as the basis and foundation of government,' it is enumerated with equal solemnity, or rather with studied emphasis. Either then, we must say, that the will of the Legislature is the only measure of their authority; or that in the plenitude of their authority, they may sweep away all our fundamental rights; or that they are bound to leave this particular right untouched and sacred. Either we must say, that they may control the freedom of the press; may abolish the trial by jury; may swallow up the Executive and Judiciary powers of the State; nay, that they may annihilate our very right of suffrage, and erect themselves into an independent and hereditary Assembly; or we must say that they have no authority to enact into a law the bill under consideration.

"We, the subscribers, say, that the General Assembly of this Commonwealth have no such authority; and that no effort on our part may be omitted against so dangerous a usurpation, we oppose to it this remonstrance; earnestly praying, as we are in duty bound, that the Supreme Lawgiver of the Universe, by illuminating those to whom it is addressed, may, on the one hand, turn aside their counsels from every act which would affront his holy prerogative, or vio-

* Dictation of Rights, in the State Constitution.

late the trust committed to them; and on the other, guide them into every measure which may be worthy of his blessing, may redound to their own praise, and may establish more firmly the liberties, the prosperity, and the happiness of this Commonwealth."*

Such as shown by their memorials, were unmistakably, the positions of the various denominations, on the several questions pending before the Legislature of 1785, in Virginia. The Episcopalians adhered to the State Establishment, and earnestly urged its continuance and support by the government, entreating the Legislature to administer a suitable rebuke to those who so pertinaciously sought its overthrow. The Methodists seconded the claims of the Episcopalians with all their might. The Presbyterians were in favor of a State Establishment of religion, but so modified as that, instead of constituting any one denomination as the State Religion, to make all orthodox denominations—the Episcopalian, the Methodist, the Presbyterian, and the Baptist—equally and alike, the Religion of the State, and advocated the support of them all by taxes assessed upon all the people, and collected, and paid over to them by the government. To all these schemes the Baptists opposed a most strenuous resistance. On the main subject, they stood alone as they had always done, but were not abashed on that account, nor the less firmly determined to pursue their object until they were crowned with success, or until they were convinced that their attainment was impracticable.

* Semple's History of the Virginia Baptists, pp. 435—444.

CHAPTER XV.

TRIUMPH OF RELIGIOUS LIBERTY IN VIRGINIA.

Defeat of the bill Establishing a Provision for the Teachers of Religion. Passage of the law Establishing Religious Freedom. History of that law. Its provisions. Opinions of it by Episcopalians and Methodists. Passage of the law Incorporating the Episcopal Church. Repeal of that law. Passage of a law repealing all laws in Relation to the State Church, and by which it ceased to be the State Church. Sale of the glebes.

THE Legislature of 1785 assembled. The several questions to which we have referred as pending were introduced. The expected conflict began. The battle was long and arduous. The bill Establishing a Provision for the Teachers of Religion—in other words, the new form proposed for a State Establishment of Religion—was put upon its passage; its friends and its opponents were intensely interested; arguments on both sides were exhausted; the memorials of the Episcopalians, Methodists, Presbyterians, and Baptists were read and heard with attention; the question was taken; the bill was defeated by a large majority. In this result the Baptists gained yet another glorious victory; the more glorious, because they here stood alone, all the other denominations being against them, and because in this case Patrick Henry forsook them, and headed the Presbyterian scheme, which, as has been said, probably owed its paternity to him. The Baptists were now full of confidence in the complete success of their

political principles, and pressed on with every assurance
to final triumph.

Lest, however, it should be thought that too much is
claimed in this case for the Baptists, the testimony of
their opponents themselves may be introduced as conclusive. Rev. Dr. Hawks, the Episcopal writer, speaking of the defeat of the bill, says:

"The Baptists were the principal promoters of this
work, and, in truth, did more than any other denomination in its accomplishment."

Speaking of the course of the Presbyterians in relation to this bill, and also the bill Establishing Religious
Liberty in Virginia, subsequently adopted, Dr. Hawks
adds:

"There can be little doubt that the distinguished individual [Mr. Jefferson], who was the leader in securing the adoption of the measures already detailed, entertained the belief that it would be no difficult task
to complete at a future session the work he had begun;
and to negative the plan of a general assessment for the
support of Christianity; nor would his expectations in
this particular have been disappointed, but for a circumstance recorded by himself, as having interposed
obstacles. In his chief object, that of giving a death-
blow to the legalized superiority of the Establishment
over all other denominations of Christians, he was cordially supported by a large body of allies who belonged
to the dissenting interests; but when that great end
was once attained [the weakening of the Establishment
by taking away the pecuniary support of the State],
and every religious society stood upon the same level,

the question in dispute assumed to these [Presbyterian] allies a very different aspect, and they deserted the standard under which they had before achieved their victory. They had prostrated the Church; they had proved themselves not at all reluctant to strip her clergy of that important maintenance which was secured to them by the possession of property [the glebes]; but they now manifested an aversion more natural than consistent, to being left to find a precarious support for themselves, in the tender mercies of a set of voluntary contributors; and the manner, almost approaching to querulousness, in which this desertion is recorded [by him], accompanied as it is by an insinuation as to the motives of the deserters, justifies the suspicion that the desertion was felt to be ungenerous. The impartial reader of a future day will probably conclude that it was a game not unskillfully played in which the troops outwitted the general. The Baptist historian boasts [and, as Dr. Hawks admits, not without reason, from the facts in the case,] that they alone were uniform in their efforts to destroy the system of an assessment, and introduce the plan of voluntary contributions; that in other denominations there was much division of sentiment between ministers and people; and that remonstrance came at last from none but the Baptists." *

The relations of the Presbyterian Church to this new plan of a State Religion, which consisted in establishing four denominations instead of one, and supporting the ministers of them all, needs some further state-

* History of the Prot. Ep. Church in Virginia, pp. 151, 152, 153.

ments to place that question beyond the reach of any future dispute, since it has lately been affirmed that they, as well as the Baptists, did remonstrate against the whole system of measures looking to that end, and that, therefore, the "boast of the Baptists," that they stood alone, is not justified by the facts in the case. Let, then, all these facts be fully stated.

Have we not seen that the Hanover Presbytery, which then embraced most of the Presbyterians in the State, in its elaborately prepared memorial, conceded, if it did not claim, the legitimacy of legislation by the State as to the temporalities of the Church; that this was necessary for the preservation of society and good government, which propositions were denied and refuted by the Baptists in their memorial; that they prayed that the scheme of assessment, if the State should decide to adopt one, might be arranged on the most liberal plan; and that this body proceeded to submit a plan to the Legislature, "agreeably to which alone," it affirmed, "Presbytery are willing to admit a general assessment for the support of religion." The discussions of the year had revealed to the Hanover Presbytery the unpopularity of the position they had assumed. It took the alarm. Efforts were made at its next session to induce it to recede from its position of the last year. It did so by resolution, but it was now too late. Its memorial was before the world, and the ends it sought had all been fairly defeated. To recede now might have been very wise, but was certainly not very timely.

The Presbyterians also adopted another expedient

to turn aside the odium of their measures. Dr. Foote says: " By invitation, signed by the ministers and several private members," a Convention was called to consider these matters. This Convention assembled at Bethel, August 10th, 1785, and " Protested against all assessments by law for religious purposes, and all incorporations of religious denominations."* But this proceeding was wholly unofficial. It was not a Presbytery, a Synod, nor a General Assembly, but simply a Convention. It did not, therefore, represent the sentiments of the Presbyterian Church, but proved only that there were Presbyterians who did not concur in political sentiment with the Hanover Presbytery. Of these doings, that Presbytery could afterwards, if it saw proper, either claim the credit, or disavow the responsibility, as future events should show to be most for its interests. It was a cautious and politic measure. Doubtless the Episcopalians could have assembled a Convention which would have adopted precisely the same measures. But would they have expressed the sentiments of the Episcopal Church? Surely not. This retrocession, however, from the position assumed in their memorial, and this protest of their Convention, remained a " dead letter." Neither was ever communicated to the Legislature. Officially they were in favor of the " Law Establishing a Provision for the Teachers of the Christian Religion." Unofficially they were against it. They contradicted and nullified themselves.

Mr. Jefferson, therefore, was right in his statements

* Foote's Sketches of Virginia, pp. 341, 344.

in regard to the proceedings of the Presbyterians on this subject; Dr. Hawks was also right; and it follows that Dr. Semple's declaration is true, that at last the Baptists were the only remonstrants against this measure, and that, as to the churches, they achieved this great victory alone, and unaided by any other denomination.

After the defeat of this bill, came up the proposed "Law Establishing Religious Freedom." This law had its origin, as we have seen, in the General Association of the Baptists of Virginia, at its session in 1777, eight years before its adoption by the General Assembly. A project was that year laid before the Legislature by Mr. Ford, but did not engage the deliberations of the body. At the session for 1779, a more perfect form of the same law—prepared at the instance of Mr. Ford, by Mr. Jefferson and Mr. Madison, during the session of the preceding Legislature—was submitted to the General Association, considered and approved, and its adoption by the State regularly urged every year thereafter, until 1785, when it became a law. Of his connection with this law, Mr. Jefferson himself gives the following account:

" Early in the session of 1776, to which I returned, (from Congress) I moved and presented a bill for the Revision of the laws, which was passed on the 24th of October, and on the 6th of November, Mr. Pendleton, Mr. Wythe, George Mason, Thomas L. Lee, and myself were appointed a committee to execute the work. We agreed to meet in Fredericksburg, to settle

18

the plan of operations, and to distribute the work. We met there accordingly, on the 18th of January, 1777. The first question was, whether we should propose to abolish the whole existing system of laws, and prepare a new and complete Institute, or preserve the general system, and only modify it to suit the present state of things." The latter plan was adopted. Soon afterwards Mr. Mason resigned his place as a member of the committee, and Mr. Lee died. These events left only three men to carry forward the design. Mr. Jefferson continues :

"We were employed in the work from that time to February, 1779, when we met in Williamsburg ; that is to say, Mr. Pendleton, Mr. Wythe, and myself; and meeting day by day, we examined critically our several parts, sentence by sentence, scrutinizing and amending, until we had agreed upon the whole. We then returned home ; had fair copies made of our several parts, which were reported to the General Assembly, January the 18th, 1779, by Mr. Wythe and myself, Mr. Pendleton's residence being distant, and he having authorized us by letter to declare his approbation.

"We had, into this work, brought so much of the Common Law as it was thought necessary to alter ; all the British Statutes from Magna Charta to the present day ; and all the laws of Virginia, from the establishment of our Legislature in the 4th of James I, to the present time, which we thought should be retained ; within the compass of a hundred and sixty-six bills, making a printed folio of ninety pages only. Some bills were taken out occasionally, from time to time, and passed. But the main body of the work was not entered upon by the Legislature, until after the general peace in 1785, when by the unwearied exertions of Mr. Madison, in opposition to the endless quibbles, chicaneries, perversions, vexations, and delays of lawyers and demi-lawyers, most of the bills were passed by the Legislature with little alteration.

"The 'Bill for Establishing Religious Freedom,' the principles of which had to a certain degree been enacted before, I had drawn in all the latitude of reason and right. It still met with opposition, but with some mutilations of the preamble, it was finally passed," "December, 1785, more than six years after it had been first reported to the House." *

Putting all these facts together we have a sufficiently clear history of the "Bill for Establishing Religious Freedom." Its substance was involved in "The Declaration of Principles by the General Association of the Baptists of Virginia, in 1775; it was submitted in the form of a protest, in 1777; it was put into proper form for Mr. Ford, the Commissioner of the Association, by Mr. Jefferson, with the assistance of Mr. Madison, in 1778; it was submitted to the General Association, read and approved, and that approval published in the minutes and in the Gazette, and afterwards moved in the Legislature in 1779; it met with such opposition as to delay its passage for six years; when it was pressed to a final adoption 'by the unwearied exertions of Mr. Madison.'"

* Jefferson's Works, vol. i., pp. 34–36.

The kind of opposition with which this law had to contend, may be imagined by referring to recorded opinions of it by several religious writers. Dr. Hawks, for example, ignorant of the fact that it was a Baptist measure; and not knowing that Mr. Jefferson and Mr. Madison cultivated the most intimate relations with the Baptist ministers, such as Williams, Walker, Waller, Ford, Leland, and others, and had been accustomed for years to send for them and others of a kindred character, or to visit them for consultation on this subject; and desirous especially to stigmatize this law as an emanation of Mr. Jefferson's supposed infidelity, remarks:—

"An act was passed by the Legislature of 1785, which was viewed by many as subversive, in its declarations, of the Christian religion, and called forth at the time, the severest animadversions of some who still reverenced the faith of the apostles. This was 'The Act for Establishing Religious Freedom,' and preceded by a memorial from the pen of Mr. Madison, which is supposed to have led to the passage of the bill." *

Thus it will be seen that to this bill especially, as has before been said—and not particularly, as stated by Benedict and others, the bill Establishing a provision for the Teachers of Religion—that the Baptist memorial of this session had reference. It might possibly have been, and probably was read on both occasions, and while it defeated the latter secured the adoption, as affirmed by Mr. Jefferson and Dr. Hawks, of the former. It is well known that when the General Committee of

---

* Hist. Prot. Ep. Ch. in Va., pp. 173, 174.

the Baptists of Virginia, following the example of the General Association, had issued its Declaration of Principles, which was simply a repetition of that adopted twelve years before by its predecessor, this Declaration was placed in the hands of Mr. Madison with a request that he would embody it in their behalf, in a memorial to the Legislature, to be issued when their great measure, "The Act for Establishing Religious Freedom," should come up before that body. These proceedings occurred in August, 1785. The Legislature assembled in October of the same year, two months afterwards. Meanwhile the address, large extracts from which have been presented in previous chapters, had been written, numerously signed, and sent to the capital. The bill had been, from the time that it was prepared, delayed eight years, and six after it was reported to the Legislature, "by lawyers, demi-lawyers," and clergymen who believed it "subversive of the Christian religion," and who, as Mr. Jefferson affirms, employed for that purpose "endless quibbles, chicaneries, and perversions." The Bill was put upon its passage in December. The forces for and against it were arrayed in all their strength. The conflict was long and obstinate. The Baptist memorial was read by Mr. Madison, who put forth all his great powers in its support. The question was demanded. The bill passed by a very large majority. The Baptists and their friends were in raptures. Their great victory was achieved. Christians in Virginia of all classes were henceforth free.

In these, and other facts in this connection, an ex-

18*

planation is found of some things which have heretofore been floating on the surface of literature and in religious society, in the somewhat intangible form of general rumor. Not a few writers have referred to them in about the same terms. They have told us, that Mr. Jefferson was in the habit of attending the meetings of a Baptist Church which worshiped in the vicinity of his residence, and of closely observing its polity especially, which was of course conducted openly, and that he afterwards said to his friends, that many of his ideas as to what a republic should be, were derived from the government of that church. In his late admirable work on "The Progress of Baptist Principles," Dr. Curtis assures us, that Mrs. Madison testified that he so stated to her. However this may be, it is unquestionably true, as many yet living aver, that Mr. Jefferson was accustomed freely to confess to his associates, and especially to Baptists, ministers and others, that the Baptist doctrines on that subject had enlightened and fixed his principles in relation to religious freedom. No one, it is presumed, can calmly contemplate the facts now submitted, and seriously question the truth of this general statement.

Any one who has read the "Declaration of Principles on Political Subjects," by the General Association of the Baptists of Virginia, and of the General Committee which succeeded it, and their various memorials, petitions, and remonstrances, addressed to the Convention and to the Legislature of the State, and has compared them with this law, must see their exact similarity in their substance, and, in many instances, even

in language. This identity could not have been acci-
dental. Irrespective of the facts in the case, which
have been stated, every intelligent man must see that
the one is the result of the other. The main features
of the law are as follows:

" *Whereas*, Almighty God hath created the mind
free; that all attempts to influence it by temporal
punishments, or burdens, or civil incapacitations, tend
only to beget habits of hypocrisy and meanness, and
are a departure from the plan of the holy Author of
our religion, who being Lord both of body and mind,
yet chose not to propagate it by coercion on either, as
was in his almighty power to do; and the impious presumption of legislators and rulers, civil as well as
ecclesiastical, who being themselves but fallible and
uninspired men, have assumed dominion over the faith
of others, setting up their own opinions and modes of
thinking as the only true and infallible, and as such
endeavoring to impose them on others, have established
and maintained false religions over the greater part of
the world, and through all time; that to compel a
man to furnish contributions of money for the propagation of opinions which he disbelieves, is sinful and
tyrannical; or even to force him to support this or that
teacher of his own religious persuasion is depriving
him of the comfortable liberty of giving his contributions to the particular pastor whose morals he would
make his pattern, and whose powers he feels most per-
suasive to righteousness; and is withdrawing from the
ministry those temporary rewards which, proceeding
from an approbation of their personal conduct, are an

additional incitement to earnest and unremitting labors for the instruction of mankind; that our civil rights have no dependence upon our religious opinions, any more than on our opinions on physics or geometry; that therefore the proscribing any citizen as unworthy the public confidence by laying upon him an incapacity of being called to offices of trust and emolument, unless he profess or renounce this or that religious opinion, is depriving him injuriously of those privileges and advantages to which, in common with his fellow-citizens, he has a natural right; that it tends only to corrupt the principles of that religion it was meant to encourage by bribing with monopoly of worldly honors and emoluments those who will externally profess and conform to it; that though, indeed, those are criminal who do not withstand such temptations, yet neither are those innocent who lay the bait in their way; that to suffer the civil magistrate to intrude his powers into the field of opinion, and to restrain the propagation or profession of principles, on supposition of their ill tendency, is a dangerous fallacy, which at once destroys all religious liberty, because he, being of course the judge of that tendency, will make his opinion the rule of his judgment, and approve or condemn the sentiments of others only as they shall square with or differ from his own; that it is time enough for the rightful purposes of civil government, for its officers to interfere when principles break out into overt acts against peace and good order; and finally, that 'Truth is great, and will prevail,' if left to herself; that she is the proper antagonist of error, and has nothing to fear from the conflict, unless

by human interposition disarmed of her natural wea-
pons, free argument and debate; errors ceasing to be
dangerous when she is permitted freely to contradict
them;

"Be it enacted by this General Assemby, that no
man shall be compelled to frequent or support any
religious worship, place, or ministry whatsoever; nor
shall he be enforced or restrained, molested or bur-
dened, in his body or goods, nor shall otherwise suffer
on account of his religious opinions or belief; but
that all men shall be free to profess, and by argument
to maintain their opinions in matters of religion; and
that the same shall in no wise diminish, enlarge, or
affect their civil capacities;" "and that we do declare
that the rights hereby asserted, are the natural rights
of mankind." *

Another law was passed by the Legislature of 1785,
the introduction of which in that form was not antici-
pated, and which in its tenor and design, was in contradiction of all its recent acts. Its leading provisions
are as follows :—

" *Whereas,* The clergy of the Protestant Episcopal
Church, by their petitions presented, have requested
that their church may be incorporated :

"Be it enacted by the General Assembly, that every
minister of the Protestant Episcopal Church now
holding a parish within this Commonwealth, either by
appointment from a vestry, or induction from a Governor, and all the vestrymen in the different parishes
now instituted, or which may hereafter be instituted

* Code of Virginia, p. 360.

within this Commonwealth, that is to say, the ministers and vestrymen of each parish respectively, or in
case of a vacancy, the vestry of each parish, and their
successors forever, are hereby made a body corporate
and politic;" it goes on to enumerate the usual powers conferred on incorporations, and gave each vestry
with its ministers, authority "to hold property not
exceeding in annual income eight hundred pounds;"
[about four thousand dollars] placed it in a position
to sue and be sued; to hold and occupy the glebe
lands; and generally to enjoy nearly all the advantages which they formerly possessed as the Established
Church of the State.*

The friends of equal religious rights seem not to
have been prepared to give any suitable resistance to
this bill; in its favor, Patrick Henry exerted all his
great powers and influence; and it became a law!

The succeeding session of the Baptist General Committee was held, commencing August 5th, 1786, at
Anderson's in Buckingham County. Mr. Ford, its
commissioner to the Legislature, made his report. He
said:

"He had waited on the House of Assembly according to appointment; that the bill Establishing Religious Freedom had passed into a law; that the bill
Establishing a Provision for the Teachers of the
Christian Religion, otherwise incorporating all the
churches, and thus making them the religion of the
State, had been defeated; and that an act "Incorporating the Protestant Episcopal Church had been

---

* Hening's Statutes at Large, vol. xi. p. 532.

adopted, nearly replacing it in its former condition, and securing to them, in the possession of the glebes, a vast amount of property rightly belonging to the State, and thus giving them many and great advantages over the Christians of other denominations."

The General Committee, in view of this report, unanimously adopted, after mature deliberation, the following resolution, the provisions of which they carried out with their usual energy:

"*Resolved*, That petitions ought to be drawn up, and circulated in the different counties [for the signatures of the people], and presented to the next General Assembly, praying for the repeal of the 'Act Incorporating the Protestant Episcopal Church;' and that the property vested in that church by this act, be sold, and the money applied to the public use."

Petitions were prepared, and approved by the body; they were placed in the hands of ministers and others; and Reuben Ford and John Leland were appointed to superintend them, and to act as commissioners to the General Assembly.

In these movements the Baptists were warmly seconded by the Presbyterians. The whole State was soon profoundly agitated. The current of feeling turned strongly against Mr. Henry, who, as a candidate before the people for a seat in the ensuing Legislature, was beaten by a very ordinary man. The remainder of the story is told by Dr. Hawks, the Episcopal historian, with sufficient distinctness. He says:

"The efforts of the Presbyterians and Baptists to

procure memorials to be presented to the Legislature
for a repeal of the act incorporating the church, and
for the distribution of its property for the public bene-.
fit, have already been recorded. The Convention [of
the Episcopal Church] was not insensible to the danger
to be apprehended from the deep-seated hostility of
these two denominations, and therefore prepared a petition to the Legislature, to counteract the effect of
their memorials, and recommended to the several parishes to prepare and present petitions of a similar
character. But all was in vain. In the next session
of the General Assembly of Virginia which succeeded
the Convention, these memorials and petitions were
brought up for consideration, and on the 5th of December, 1786, the House of Delegates, among other
resolutions, adopted the following:

" 'That the Act for Incorporating the Protestant
Episcopal Church ought to be repealed.'

"On the 9th of January, 1787, the bill to carry into
effect this resolution was passed by the Senate, and
thus became the law of Virginia." *

The Annual Session of the General Committee of
the Baptists of Virginia for 1787, was held, commencing on the 10th day of August, at Dover, in Goochland County. This session was memorable for the
final measures which completed the reunion of all
classes of Baptists then in Virginia. On this subject
Dr. Benedict says:

"The schism which took place among the Regular
and Separate Baptists in 1766," "had continued with-

---

* History of the Protestant Episcopal Church in Va., p. 194.

out being completely healed for about twenty years, although a very friendly intercourse had been" "kept up among them. But in 1787 the happy period arrived in which all disputes between these two bodies were compromised, buried, and forgotten." * This reunion was the more easy to obtain, and the more happy and effectual, because it was sought in the midst of a great and glorious revival among all the Baptist churches, which continued to prevail until near the close of that century.

Mr. Ford and Mr. Leland reported verbally. They said: "That according to their instructions they presented the memorial entrusted to them to the Legislature; that in compliance with their petitions, the 'Act Incorporating the Protestant Episcopal Church' was repealed; but that the Glebe laws still remained untouched, and in full force."

These splendid estates, so numerous and so valuable, were still in the hands of the Episcopal clergy, who were living upon them in princely style. Their restoration to the State, and sale to diminish the burden of the public debt, alone remained, and the Baptists would have gained all the objects they ever sought at the hands of the State government. This they found to be their most difficult work. Long was its accomplishment delayed; and often were they foiled in their attempts; but never for a moment did they lose sight of their object or relax their exertions, until success crowned their indefatigable endeavors.

Again the General Committee adopted resolutions

* History, &c., vol. ii, pp. 60, 61.

19

declaring the glebes public property, and that they ought to be sold, and the proceeds applied to public purposes. A memorial to this end was reported and adopted, and immense numbers of signatures of the people obtained, and Eleazer Clay, Reuben Ford, John Waller, and John Williams were appointed commissioners to lay it before the Legislature, and obtain, if possible, their purpose. They met with no success. The next year the same process was repeated, and Leland, Waller, and Clay were appointed commissioners, but the result was the same as at the previous session. Each year, for eleven years, they continued undiscouraged—though failing in every instance—to memorialize and petition the Legislature. In 1799, their address was favorably received and considered, and the following bill was introduced and adopted, "Entitled an Act to Repeal certain Acts, and to Declare the Construction of the Bill of Rights and the Constitution Concerning Religion:

"Whereas, the Constitution of the State of Virginia hath pronounced the Government of the King of England to have been totally dissolved by the Revolution; hath substituted in place of the government so dissolved, a new Civil Government; and hath in the Bill of Rights, excepted from the powers given to the substituted government, the power of reviving any species of Ecclesiastical or church government in lieu of that dissolved, by referring the subject of religion to the conscience; and

"Whereas, the several acts presently recited, do admit the church established under the Regal government to have been continued so, subsequently to the Constitution; have bestowed property upon that church; have asserted a legislative right to establish any religious sect and have incorporated religious sects; all of which is inconsistent with the principles of the Constitution and of Religious Freedom, and manifestly tends to the re-establishment of a National Church; for remedy whereof,

"Be it enacted," and the law proceeds to describe and repeal the several acts of 1776, of 1779, of 1785, of 1786, and of 1788; and to declare that "The Act Establishing Religious Freedom contains the true construction of the Bill of Rights, and of the Constitution."*

This law swept away the last vestiges of the Established Church; it annihilated all pretence of authority to restore it, or to establish by law or incorporate to be supported by the State, any form of religion, or any church or churches whatever; and it alienated all the glebes; but it left them still in the hands of the Episcopal clergy, and neither ordered their sale nor occupancy by the State. The Baptists were not satisfied, and continued to memorialize, remonstrate, and petition the Legislature, which by the law of January 12th, 1802, completed the work. That law is as follows:—

"Whereas, The General Assembly on the 24th day of January, 1799, by their act of that date, repealed all the laws relative to the late Protestant Episcopal Church, and declared a true exposition of the Bill of Rights and Constitution, respecting the same, to be

---

* Laws of Virginia, edition 1803, p. 388.

contained in the act entitled 'An act for Establishing Religious Freedom,' thereby recognizing the principle that all property formerly belonging to the said church, of every description, devolved on the good people of this Commonwealth on the dissolution of the British Government here, in the same degree in which the right and interest of the said church was derived from them.

"Be it therefore enacted," and the General Assembly proceeds to order the sale of the glebes, and the application of the funds arising, all of which in due time was carried into full effect.

In 1786, the Presbyterians acted with the Baptists in this work. They then withdrew, and from that time the Baptists were emphatically alone. The testimony of Dr. Hawks on this point is important. Speaking of the decision of the Baptist General Committee in 1787, he says:—*

"That vote decided the fate of the glebes." And in another place:—"After the final success of the Baptists [in defeating the bill Establishing a Provision for the Teachers of the Christian Religion, in securing the adoption of the law Establishing Religious Freedom, and various other similar measures] their next efforts were to procure the sale of the church lands, and their efforts never ceased until the glebes were sold."

In another place, speaking of the Baptists, he says: "The war which they waged against the Church was a war of extermination. They seem to have known no

* Hist. Prot. Ep. Ch. Va., pp. 121, 122, 137, 138, 152, 153.

relentings, and their hostility never ceased for seven and twenty years. They revenged themselves for their sufferings [at the hands of the Establishment] by the almost total ruin of the Church."

The last battle had now been fought, and the victory of the Baptists was complete. Nothing more could reasonably be desired. The Government of Virginia, in all dealings with religious questions had taken ground which was thoroughly Baptist. The former vigilance was no longer necessary, and the General Committee—"The Standing Sentinel on Political Subjects"—which on account of several of its acts infringing the rights of the churches, had elicited their jealousy, was, in 1799, dissolved. As a centre of brotherly intercourse merely, an organization was formed under the name of the General Meeting of Correspondence, which twenty years after gave place to the purely missionary body, now known as the General Association of Virginia.

The war with England, into which all the Baptists entered so heartily, and their increasing excitement on political subjects naturally withdrew their minds to a great extent from religion. A painful spiritual dearth came over the churches. It was hardly possible that it could have been otherwise. When, however, peace returned to the country, and most of their political purposes had been gained, a new spirit and life were diffused among the people, and a glorious revival spread throughout the whole State. Dr. Benedict says of it:—

"This work, which was powerful and extensive,

19*

began on the banks of James River, in 1785, and thence spread, like fire among stubble, in all directions," "and as it continued for several years, there were very few churches which were not visited with its salutary influence." "It continued spreading until thousands were converted and baptized, besides many who joined the Methodists and Presbyterians. The Episcopalians, although much dejected at the loss of the Establishment, had nevertheless continued their public worship, and were attended by respectable congregations. But after this revival their society fell fast into dissolution." The Baptists "were joined by persons of much greater weight in civil society" than formerly. "Their congregations became more numerous than those of any other Christian sect, and they may from this period be considered as taking the lead in matters of religion." *

* History of the Baptists, vol. 2, pp. 90, 91, 92.

CHAPTER XVI.

INFLUENCE OF THE EARLY BAPTISTS OF VIRGINIA IN THE FORMATION OF THE GENERAL GOVERNMENT.

Incidental influence. Direct influence. Objections to the Federal Constitution. Correspondence of the General Committee with Washington. Amendment to the Constitution. Its acceptance by the Baptists.

INCIDENTAL allusions have been made in previous chapters to the influence of the Early Baptists of Virginia in the formation of the General Government. In fixing the character of the Federal Constitution, their influence was powerfully felt, since it was exerted indirectly through the medium of their friends, and directly through appeals and addresses. The objects which they sought, were fully and satisfactorily accomplished.

In the great work which they had accomplished in Virginia, the Baptists, as we have seen, had, as their coadjutors, the ablest politicians in the State. These very men were now in the councils of the nation that formed the Constitution of the United States. That Constitution, as at first published, failed to meet the expectation of the Baptists of Virginia. The sixth article provided as follows :—

" No religious test shall ever be required as a qualification to any office or public trust, under the United States."

To persons less jealous and vigilant, this might have seemed, and did seem to General Washington for example, sufficient. The Baptists had suffered too much to be content with a reference to that subject so slight and indefinite. In their opinion, it was radically defective in plain, full, and direct declaration. It was proposed by Mr. Pinckney of South Carolina, and even this was resisted by Mr. Sherman of Connecticut, who preferred that the Constitution should not refer to religion at all, maintaining that "the prevailing liberality was a sufficient security against such tests."* Mr. Sherman's State it was well known, retained its "Established Order" which was supported by a tax upon all the people, Baptists as well as others. These circumstances were suspicious. And besides, it did not, in so many words, affirm that no national religion should ever be established; it did not guaranty to every citizen equal protection in his person, his property, and all his rights, irrespective of his faith and worship; it did not declare that no one religious denomination should ever, in any respect, be preferred above another; it did not disavow the right of the government ever to interfere with religion in any form; it only gave an assurance that "No religious *test* should ever be required as a *qualification to any office,* or public trust under the United States."

The General Committee of the Baptists of Virginia, for 1788, assembled March the 7th, at Williams', in Goochland County. Before entering upon the subject of education, which occupied much of its attention at

* Madison Papers, vol. 3, p. 1468.

that meeting, the following question was submitted for its decision :—

" Does the new Federal Constitution, which has now lately made its appearance in public, make sufficient provision for the secure enjoyment of religious liberty?"

The question was entertained ; the Constitution was read ; and the whole subject fully and ably discussed. The question was then put to vote, and decided unanimously in the negative.*

The inquiry now arose as to what in this exigency was proper to be done. On motion, a committee was appointed to prepare an address to General Washington on the subject, and to correspond with Baptists in other States, especially in Massachusetts, Rhode Island, and New York, and to obtain if practicable, their concurrence and co-operation, in obtaining such amendments to the Constitution of the General Government as might render it acceptable. At the head of this committee was placed the distinguished John Leland.   It was instructed to report at the next Annual Meeting.

The session of the General Committee for 1789, was held during the first week in August, in the city of Richmond. Mr. Leland had leave to report, and presented to the Committee copies of correspondence, and the proposed address to General Washington. The correspondence, if it has been preserved, is among the papers of Mr. Reuben Ford, or of Robert B. Semple, D. D., in the hands of their descendants, and to us inaccessible. The address was read, considered,

* Semple's Hist. Va. Bapt., pp. 76, 77.

adopted, signed officially, and transmitted to the President. We make the following extracts:—

"The General Committee of the United Baptist Churches in Virginia, assembled in the city of Richmond, August 8th, 1789, to the President of the United States :—

" Sir, Among the many congratulations which you receive from societies, cities, States, and the whole country, we wish to offer ours, &c. ; " and after enumerating various considerations, the address then proceeds :—

"The want of efficacy in the Confederation [without a General Government, extending over the whole country] the redundancy of laws in the States, and their partial administration, called aloud for a new arrangement of our system. The wisdom of the States for that purpose was collected in a Grand Convention over which you, Sir, had the honor to preside. A National Government in all its parts was recommended as the only preservative of the Union, which plan of Government is now in actual operation.

" When the Constitution first made its appearance in Virginia, as a Society, we had unusual struggles of mind, fearing that the liberty of conscience, dearer to us than property or life, was not sufficiently secured. Perhaps our jealousies were heightened by the usage we received in Virginia under the Regal Government, when mobs, bonds, fines, and prisons were our frequent repasts. We are convinced on the one hand that without an effective National Government, the States would fall into disunion, and all the consequent evils; and on the other we fear should we give this Constitution our assent, that we should be accessory to some religious oppression should any one society in the Union preponderate over all the rest, and get possession of the Government, which is very possible, and against which no provision is made; we have voted unanimously that the Constitution does not make sufficient provision for the secure enjoyment of religious liberty.

"Amidst all these inquietudes, our consolation arises from the consideration that the plan bears the signature of a tried and trusty friend, in whose opinion it must be good; and that if religious liberty is rather insecure in the Constitution, the Administration will certainly prevent all oppression; for a Washington will preside.

"May that Divine Munificence that covered your head in battle, make you a yet greater blessing to your admiring country in time of peace. Should the horrid evils that have been so pestiferous in Asia and Europe—faction, ambition, war, perfidy, fraud, and persecutions for conscience' sake—ever approach the borders of our happy nation, may the name and administration of our beloved President, like the radiant source of day, scatter all those dark clouds from the American hemisphere. And while we thus speak freely the language of our own hearts, we are satisfied that we express the sentiments of our brethren whom we represent." "It is our prayer to Almighty God, that the Federal Government and the Government of the respective States, without rivalship, may so co-operate together as to make the numerous people over whom you preside the happiest nation on earth, and you, Sir, the happiest man, in seeing a people whom, by the smiles of Providence you saved from vassalage by your martial valor, and made wise by your maxims, sitting securely under their vines and fig trees, enjoying the perfection of human felicity.

" May God long preserve your life and health for a blessing to the world in general, and to the United States in particular ; and when, like the sun, you have finished your course of great and unequalled services, and you go the way of all the earth, may the Divine Being who will reward every man according to his works, grant unto you a glorious admission into his everlasting kingdom, through Jesus Christ our Lord."

To this address Washington returned promptly the following autograph reply:

"To the General Committee representing the United Baptists of Virginia:

"Gentlemen:—I request that you will accept my best acknowledgments for your congratulations on my appointment to the first office in the nation.   The kind manner in which you mention my past conduct, equally claims the expression of my gratitude.

"After we had, by the smiles of Divine Providence on our exertions, obtained the object for which we contended, I retired, at the conclusion of the war, with an idea that my country could have no further occasion for my services, and with the intention of never entering again into public life.   But when the exigencies of my country seemed to require me once more to engage in public affairs, an honest conviction of duty superceded my former resolution, and became my apology for deviating from the happy plan which I had adopted.

"If I could have entertained the slightest apprehension that the Constitution planned by the Convention where I had the honor to preside, might possibly endanger the religious rights of any Ecclesiastical Society, certainly I never would have placed my signature to it; and if I could now conceive that the General Government might ever be so administered as to render the liberty of conscience insecure, I beg you will be persuaded that no one would be more zealous than myself to establish effectual barriers against the horrors of spiritual tyranny, and every species of religious persecution.

"You doubtless remember, for I have often expressed my sentiments, that every man conducting himself as a good citizen, and being accountable to God alone for his religious opinions, ought to be protected in worshipping the Deity according to the dictates of his own conscience. Whilst I recollect with satisfaction that the religious society of which you are members, has been throughout America, uniformly and almost unanimously, the firm friends of civil liberty, and the persevering promoters of our religious revolution, I cannot hesitate to believe that they will be faithful supporters of a free yet efficient General Government.

"Under this pleasing expectation, I rejoice to assure them that they may rely upon my best wishes and endeavors to advance their prosperity. In the meantime,

20

be assured, gentlemen, that I entertain a proper sense of your fervent supplications to God for my temporal and eternal happiness."

Several developments in this correspondence ought to be noticed. We refer to them in the briefest possible terms: 1. The General Committee speak to Washington as to an old and familiar personal friend, well known to all its members, and in whose intelligence, patriotism, and integrity they have in all respects undoubting confidence. 2. Washington speaks to them in the same terms of familiar knowledge, reminding them of his often-expressed sentiments in their presence, as friends and neighbors, which, on the whole subject of religious freedom, they well knew to correspond in every respect with their own. 3. He refers to the revolution which the Baptists had effected on religious subjects in Virginia as "*our* religious revolution." 4. His compliment to the patriotism of the Baptists, as a class, not in Virginia only, but throughout America, indicates that it must have been singularly conspicuous, and, coming as it did from the Commander-in-chief of the army, whose opportunities for knowledge on the subject were so full, was honorable to them in the highest degree. 5. He expresses his belief that the Constitution he had subscribed gave sufficient guaranties for the safety of their religious rights, but declares his readiness to co-operate with them in obtaining by an amendment such further securities as might satisfy them entirely. Engaged in a cause so excellent in all its bearings, and with Washington, Jefferson, Madison, and a host of others of note not much inferior, the Baptists could not, with God's blessing, fail of accomplishing their purpose. Accordingly the amendment which became the supreme law of the United States on that subject, was proposed, and its adoption was demanded by *Virginia*. The language suggested by Virginia was as follows:

"That religion, or the duty which we owe to our Creator, and the manner of discharging it, can be directed only by reason and conviction, not by force or violence; and, therefore, all men have an equal, natural, and inalienable right to the free exercise of religion, according to the dictates of conscience, and that no particular religious sect or society ought to be favored or established by law in preference to others." *

This is unmistakable Baptist language, constantly uttered by them in this State. The form of the amendment as found in the Constitution, is as follows:

"Congress shall make no law respecting an Establishment of Religion, or prohibiting the free exercise thereof; or abridging the freedom of speech or of the press; or the right of the people peaceably to assemble, and to petition the government for a redress of grievances."

This amendment was reported to the General Committee; was received as satisfactory; and that body now expressed its cordial approval of the Constitution of the Federal Government. It contained, as did the Constitution of Virginia, embodied within itself, in the form of organic law, the peculiar doctrines of the Baptists regarding the powers of civil government in the

* Elliot's State Conventions and Debates, &c., Vol. 2, p. 485.

department of religion.   Nothing more was now wanting for the preservation of the peace, security, and per-
petuation of the nation, but a strict and faithful conformity to the Constitution on the part of the Congress,
the Judiciary, and the Federal Executive.

CHAPTER XVII.

DEFENCE OF THE EARLY BAPTISTS OF VIRGINIA.

Their position and influence. Their disinterestedness. Education of their ministers. Style and elocution of their sermons. Their defence bequeathed to their successors.

IT is matter of equal surprise and regret that the Early Baptists of Virginia have, apparently, been systematically depreciated. To this fact we have sufficiently referred in our introductory chapter. I should have performed my task unfaithfully, if before closing this brief volume, since I have set forth so fully their defects, failures, and errors, I did not also essay at least to defend them from those aspersions under which their memory has so long labored, and place them before the world in their true character. In these sketches, it must be conceded, the balances have been held with an even hand. Censure, where censure was due, has not been withheld, nor has praise been bestowed when it was not richly merited. There are those in the religious, as well as in the social and political world, who seek to elevate themselves by depressing others. The Early Baptists of Virginia have, accordingly, in certain quarters, been represented as indeed eminently religious and conscientious men, estimable in their place, but without refinement, destitute of learning, and to a great extent bigoted enthusiasts. That such was really their character, many of

20*

the present age have come fully to believe and readily to concede. How an impression so utterly unfounded, was originated, and by what means it has been kept alive among the people, are questions of easy solution by all those who will be at the pains to study the subject.

The extraordinary success with which God was pleased to crown both their spiritual and their civil labors, mortified insufferably various influential parties, who lost no opportunity, in conversation, in the pulpit, or through the press, to impugn their character and position. In this form they continued to carry on persecution against them. They could no longer fine, imprison, and scourge them, but they could still "tread them under foot with foul reproaches and most arrogant scorn," and in this process they were successful. Conscious of their integrity and power, these reproaches, this arrogant scorn, they did not deign to notice. Perhaps it was not ungrateful to them to be considered by the proud and ambitious, as were the primitive Christians, "the offscouring of all things." Defamations and aspersions of this kind remained unanswered. For the sake of the effect they were appropriated. Later writers entered into their spirit, and copied their style. It was the same thing whether they were abused as by Burk and Jarrett; misrepresented by Hawks and Rice; ignored as by Foote; or caricatured as by Alexander and Meade. Nor have men been wanting in their own ranks who thought themselves at liberty patronizingly to apologize for the deficiencies of their Ecclesiastical Fathers, such men as Thomas and Gar-

rard, Waller and Harris, Walker and Straughan, to
whom they themselves, in learning, talents, and eloquence, were as molehills by the side of "high
Olympus." Thus a form of public sentiment was
manufactured, which on account of the quarter whence
it sprung, and because it was unresisted, fixed itself
tenaciously in the literature of the times, and became
comparatively permanent. At first, for much of the
revolutionary spirit that prevailed among the masses,
and especially for those radical principles of liberty,
political and religious, so offensive to the clergy and
their friends, the Baptists were held strictly responsible. Not a few of those who subsequently sought to
appropriate to themselves the chief honors, were in
those days sufficiently prudent. They had reasons to
doubt whether the British yoke would after all be
broken; and they thought it necessary to leave themselves, in such a case, room safely to retreat. For
their own security they were especially careful. They
were not unwilling to see the Baptists throw themselves
without regard to consequences into the breach, assured
that if benefit was secured, they should share it, and
that if suffering was to be endured, they should escape
it. Had the American Revolution failed, the Baptists
in this country would undoubtedly have been involved
in obloquy as deep and as blighting as was that of
their brethren of a former age, on a similar account in
Germany. Here as well as there, "the blood of myriads would have expiated their offences." Virginia
would have been the Münster of America. It was
precisely, therefore, because they possessed in so emi-

nent a degree, intelligence, influence, and moral force, —the very qualities afterwards denied them, and for the supposed want of which they have been so long defamed,—and because they exercised these powers so successfully, that this feeling of dislike, not to say hatred, arose, and since has been cherished with so much pertinacity.

In their direct spiritual labors, in the conversion of sinners, the multiplication of churches, and the building up of the cause of Christ in Virginia, never since the days of the Apostles have any people been more successful. And how great were their achievements in the cause of political freedom! We have seen that as a body the Baptists of Virginia were the first, whether religious or political, to declare in favor of opposing an armed resistance to the usurpations of England; that in an address they urged this measure upon the State Convention, soon after assembled to consider that subject; and that the Convention accordingly instructed the delegates of the State in Congress to declare the Independence of the United States; we have seen that they succeeded in placing in the Constitution of the State, and therefore at the very foundation of the government, a summary of their principles on political government, which clearly led to all their subsequent triumphs in the department of religious freedom; that with the aid of the Presbyterians they secured the passage of the law abolishing all penalties against the exercise of freedom of opinion and worship; that with the Presbyterians, and all others against them, they alone defeated the bill which proposed to tax the peo-

ple to procure a support for the ministers of all denominations; that, aided by the Presbyterians, they obtained the repeal of the law imposing taxes upon the
people for the support of the Episcopal clergy, the repeal of the marriage law, and the adoption of the law
placing the ministers of all denominations upon the
same official footing, the repeal of the law incorporating
the Protestant Episcopal Church, and the repeal of all
the laws in relation to the Established Church of Virginia; that, after eight years' toil, they secured the
adoption of the "Law Establishing Religious Freedom;" and after more than twenty years, the law ordering the sale of the glebes, and the appropriation of
the proceeds to the payment of the public debt. They
did more. They placed a summary of their political
principles in the Federal Constitution, and, therefore,
at the very foundation of the General Government,
which led to the full establishment of religious freedom
throughout the whole country. They labored long
and anxiously. Their success was complete. Their
opponents employed every art to turn aside or to evade
their pursuit. Their ground was not relinquished until
driven from it by force, and then it was given up inch
by inch, and with the utmost reluctance. All their
movements were watched by the Baptists with sleepless
vigilance. They met them gallantly at every point,
and drove back their legions. Upon the legislative
attention they continued to press their doctrines, no
matter how frequently repulsed, until their whole purpose was completely accomplished. Were those who
did all this a class of men of whom, without making

himself ridiculous, any writer could say: They were eminently religious and conscientious men, estimable in their place, but without refinement, or position in society, destitute of learning, and, to a great extent, bigoted enthusiasts?

The idea may, however, suggest itself, that in the representations now submitted injustice has been done to the other denominations that then prevailed in the Commonwealth.   It may be answered that, unless we include the Quakers, who were very few in numbers, and as a church took no part in public affairs, there were but four denominations; the Episcopalians, the Methodists, the Presbyterians, and the Baptists. From the brow of any patriot of those "times that tried men's souls," no matter to what denomination he belonged, God forbid that we, or any one else, should pluck a single laurel.   No, let them all flourish there, ever fresh and green.   We have given, and ever will give, all "honor to whom honor is due."   That very many of all denominations—Presbyterians, and even Episcopalians and Methodists—labored nobly with the Baptists, is well known.   But it is equally well known that, except in the case of the Presbyterians, they labored as individuals, and not as churches; and even the Presbyterians themselves fell short in three or four cases, and in two or three, were in favor of legal vassalage, and in opposition to the Baptists.   We have fully sustained the truth of every statement we have made, by ample and unquestionable authorities.   To show that the Episcopal Church, and the Methodist Church, as churches, resisted earnestly, and to the end, all changes in the government, and sought by every means in their power to retain their hold upon its patronage, we will once more quote from Dr. Hawks. Referring to the Methodist Church he says:—

"They claimed to be nothing more than members of a religious society formed within the bosom of the Established Church at home, and extended to America. The language of the Methodist preachers was that 'All who left the Church, left the Methodists.' Nay, such was the avowed attachment of the Society, that in public opinion it was so far identified with the Church, as to share with it the odium which from political causes, then rested on the Establishment in Virginia. The Methodists were suspected of being inimical to the liberties of America. This suspicion in the minds of many, originated in nothing but the known adherence of the Society to an Ecclesiastical system which had the support of the civil power."*

In another place referring to the various petitions to the Legislature, already sufficiently described, Dr. Hawks says:—

"In these petitions all classes in the community joined, with the exception of Churchmen and Methodists. These sent in their petitions for the continuance of the Establishment."†

The position of the Presbyterians has been before defined with sufficient clearness. In some of the conflicts of those days, they, and especially the Hanover Presbyterians, battled nobly. In the overthrow of the colossal Establishment they fought gallantly. It is,

---

* Hist. Prot. Ep. Ch., in Va., p. 133.   † Idem, p 139.

therefore, the more a matter of surprise and regret, that they indicated a desire to be themselves established with others, as the religion of the State; and that they sought the taxation of the people, for the support of their own ministers. Truly, therefore, did Dr. Semple say of them, that "The ministry and the people were so much at variance as to paralyze all their exertions."

The Baptists throughout the whole struggle presented an unbroken front. They were calm, modest, respectful; but firm, immovable, untiring, indomitable; deterred by no onsets; disheartened by no defeats. Yet they are gravely charged, in learned and popular volumes, with being influenced in all they did by such motives only as overweening hatred to the Establishment, and an ardent zeal to advance their own interests as a sect; by a general restless and radical spirit; and as being the tools merely of political intriguers.*

All these and such like imputations, severally and as a whole, from whatever quarter, are here repelled, in the name and on behalf of the sainted dead. They were capable of being influenced by no such motives; they were impelled to action by no such feelings; they cherished no such malignity towards their fallen persecutors; no such spirit of revenge animated their proceedings; they were the tools of no such political party leaders; they sought for themselves no such peculiar advantages; they determined to share with their

---

* Hawks' History, &c., pp. 121, 122, 137, 138. Dr. John H. Rice's pamphlets. Semple's History, &c., pp. 245-254. Bishop Meade's Old Families, and Old Churches.

fellow-citizens, whether friends or opponents, and did
share with them, all the triumphs they gained of truth,
of honor, of justice, and of civil and religious liberty.
They maintained, in all that they did, no novelty, but
only those doctrines which their fathers had advocated
in every land, and for seventeen centuries, and in
defence of which had been sacrificed millions of treasure, and tens of thousands of the purest lives ever
looked upon by the sun from heaven.

The ministry especially, of the Early Baptists of
Virginia, have been reproached as having been uneducated men.

This feature is nauseously prominent in the frequent
references to them by all denominations, but by Presbyterians and Episcopalians especially. They desire
their ministry to be judged by the best specimens
among them. That of the Baptists, they insist upon
judging by the worst. Were the Baptists even of
those days indifferent to the advantages of education?
The amplest proofs to the contrary have, in a previous
chapter, been submitted. But were the Baptist ministers of those times really uneducated men? If by
education, classical learning only is meant, then not a
few of them were educated, since they were classically
learned, being graduates of colleges in this country, or
in Europe. I will not say that they were, on that
account, professionally, more learned than many others
whose literary and scientific advantages had been less
ample, but with whom they delighted to labor in the
cause of Christ. Cast your eyes along their thick and
serried ranks. Whom do you find there? Stearns,

21

Thomas, the Marshalls, Harris, the Craigs, Armstead, Baker, the Wallers, Ford, Leland, Toler, Clay, Greenwood, Nelson, Barrow, Williams, Webber, Walker, and hundreds of others. Whence came they? From the pulpits of the Episcopal, the Presbyterian, the Congregational, and other churches; from their seats in the Colonial Legislature; from the roll of officers in the army; from the chairs of instruction in the schools; from the offices of the justices and sheriffs in the counties; and from the broad fields of the wealthy planter. The strikingly illiterate among them were, perhaps, not more numerous in proportion than the incorrigibly dull of other denominations, who had been dragged through a college curriculum; and were practically fully as useful.

The great mass of Baptist ministers of that day, were, however, not classically educated. How could they have been? Where were the schools, to which they might have resorted for that purpose? They did not exist in the country. Still, their learning was not inferior to that of the best portions of the people. Were men of the other professions all classically educated? Was Patrick Henry classically educated? Were Bland, Pendleton, Carrington, classically educated? Was Washington himself classically educated? Yet who has ever reproached them as uneducated men? Professionally, they were all educated men. And professionally, the Baptist ministers of that day were educated men. Their erudition in the gospel was as profound and varied, as was that of their great contemporaries in the law and in politics. Nor were they in any sense their inferiors. The Pharisees regarded the Apostles as "unlearned, and ignorant men," and with as little reason as have Pedobaptist divines the ministry of the Early Baptists of Virginia. That they had not the theological training of that age, we have reason to be profoundly grateful, since there existed not then upon the face of the earth, an institution of this class, Papist or Protestant, the teaching of which was not radically and incurably corrupt. From the Bible alone, which they studied daily with clear heads, warm hearts, and fervent prayer for the divine guidance, they derived their theology. Of the true sense of the word of God, they therefore knew more, and could consequently better teach it, than all the doctors of the Sorbonne, of Geneva, of Wittenberg, of Oxford, or of Cambridge.

It is assumed and declared, that the sermons of these Early Baptist ministers of Virginia, were inferior in matter; that their style and elocution were repulsive; and that, even for that day, their manners, in and out of the pulpit, were rude and offensive.

That there were among them some individuals obnoxious to these imputations, and that the same was true to an equal extent in proportion to numbers, of all the other denominations, there can be no doubt. But when they are applied to them as a class, they become preposterous, defamatory, and malignant. Baptist ministers generally, destitute of learning or eloquence, shallow, rude, repulsive! Why then, it may be asked, were their discourses always heard by immense crowds, who were swayed by their strange power, and agitated to an extent never exceeded in this or any other country? Why were the splendid parish churches—whose numerous magnificent ruins stand to this day in many of the lower counties of Virginia, the mouldering monuments of colonial pride and regal extravagance—forsaken of their polished and courtly congregations, who eagerly followed these coarse, rude, plebeian preachers, and hung upon their words with rapt and delighted attention? And why did they by hundreds unite with their churches? By what unknown and unaccountable power, did these same coarse, uneducated, rude, plebeian preachers overthrow the triple-walled citadel of the Establishment, sever all the firmly established relations between Church and State; carry with them in their blind, ignorant fanaticism almost the whole people; and fix their political principles ineradicably in the government of the State and of the United States? All this they did without learning, polish, or influence, and in despite of all their ignorance, coarseness, and rude plebeian fanaticism! Contending against insuperable disadvantages, their achievements were more and greater than ever have been accomplished in any other age or country, even by the great, the mighty, and the wise! And yet these monstrous defamations have been heard and read for the last fifty years by the people, without rebuke and without contempt!

Some of these early Baptist ministers were certainly "no orators." But where is the denomination, every one of whose ministers is a Whitefield, a Hall, or a Chalmers? Have any other churches in Virginia produced ministers superior in eloquence to Stearns and Walker, Straughan and Lunsford, Andrew Broaddus and John Kerr? We say nothing of such men as Williams and Harris, Marshall and Toler, and in later times, Semple and Dabbs, Clopton and Goodall. These and such as these possessed an amount of mental vigor, of intellectual cultivation, of professional research and pulpit power, that justly placed them on a level, to say the least, with any other ministers of their day and country. If by eloquence is meant the ability to attract and please, to persuade, to move the people to action, then these were men of unsurpassed eloquence. With amazing success did they declare

> "Truths of power,
> In words immortal. Not such words as flash
> From the fierce demagogue's unthinking rage,
> To madden for a moment, and expire;
> Nor such as the rapt orator imbues
> With warmth of facile sympathy, and moulds
> To mirrors radiant with fair images,
> To grace the noble fervor of an hour;
> But words which have the spirit of great deeds
> Winged for the future."

To the Virginia Baptists of the present age, to whom we have shown who they were, what they did, and how they have been assailed, the Early Baptists of Virginia have bequeathed the custody of their illustrious name. To our fidelity they have confided their sacred honor. We have entered into their labors. We have inherited the sunny fields in which they achieved their conquests. These fields are now all radiant with golden fruit, and fragrant flowers, and resplendent beauty. Shall we prove recreant to the holy trust thus confided to our keeping? Why should we longer refrain to claim for them their just place in history, and, by a proper exhibition of the truth, drive back their unscrupulous assailants? He who can coldly, silently, heartlessly, permit their noble bearing, their generous sacrifices, their exalted deeds, to be buried in darkness or tarnished by the breath of calumny, deserves not the name of Baptist. What then shall we think of some of their degenerate sons, who assist in detracting them, and who themselves with parricidal hand essay to strike them down! They deserve, and will in due time receive, the execrations of all good men. He who is untrue to his own family, domestic or ecclesiastical, cannot be true to his God. Let no such man be trusted.

More and more precious with each passing year becomes the memory of these revered Fathers. No effective means, moral or material, will we permit to remain unimproved which may give point and impressiveness to that important lesson, commended no less by the instincts of the great universal heart than by the testimony of all experience, that any people who would hope for the blessing of God, insure their own honor, and obtain future success, must preserve as an inviolable treasure the broad ægis upon which are emblazoned the virtues and achievements of their forefathers.

THE END.

www.ingramcontent.com/pod-product-compliance
Lightning Source LLC
Chambersburg PA
CBHW030402270326
41926CB00009B/1231